The New Paradigm: Volume I

The Way Things Ought to Be *Fixed*

Income Taxes, Social Security, and Medicare

James William Tsakanikas

© 2018

Table of Contents

Introduction

The New Paradigm is a series of books whose purpose is to re-invent America by eliminating corruption and reigning in politicians while facilitating the preamble of the Constitution of the United States of America as follows:

We the People of the United States, in Order to form a more perfect Union, establish Justice, insure domestic Tranquility, provide for the common defence, promote the general Welfare, and secure the Blessings of Liberty to ourselves and our Posterity, do ordain and establish this Constitution for the United States of America.

(They really did spell defense differently back in the day.)

Some say that the real problem is spending, and some say it's a revenue problem. They are both right, but the revenue problem needs to be fixed before the spending problem. It's a chicken and egg thing. The revenue problem should be fixed first for several reasons, to name a few: 1) it's easier, 2) it's less contentious, 3) it can be implemented faster, 4) it removes a tremendous burden, 5) it actually reduces spending, and 6) it will provide the most relief. Therefore spending will be addressed in ***The New Paradigm Volume II***.

This first volume will fix the revenue side of the Income Tax System, Social Security, and Medicare while removing avenues for corruption by politicians, companies, and individuals. This volume will provide ***The Best Tax Solution*** yet devised for reforming the tax system and establish a strategy for implementing that solution. Leading up to ***The Best Tax Solution*** this book will detail the characteristics that ***The Best Tax Solution*** must posses. If a person agrees that all of the detailed characteristics are indeed required, they will agree with ***The Best Tax Solution***. Remember, Volume I only addresses the revenue side, Volume II will complete the equation.

Many books describe the problems with the current tax system and some books actually offer sincere although half-baked solutions. This volume will superficially describe the major inadequacies of the tax system, how we got to where we are at, and explore some of the more popular solutions that claim fairness, flatness, and/or simplicity. The failure of other books on this subject is their inability to articulate a strategy for implementing their pie-in-the-sky solution. What's the point in offering a solution and not specifying how to get there from the current unconscionable tax system?

Since the 16th Amendment to the United States Constitution went into effect in 1913, the Federal Government has, usually on an annual basis, formulated a new income tax scheme, usually more onerous than the last scheme. The tax scheme has grown so burdensome that it requires millions of bookkeepers, CPAs, tax attorneys, and IRS agents to administer and manage all its permutations. That does not include the billions of hours (yes billions) and billions of dollars spent by individuals and companies to prepare and comply with Internal Revenue Service laws, rules, and regulations.

This tax scheme is a massive yoke on the U.S. economy, replete with intrusive government actions and fraught with loop-holes and fraud. The tax scheme creates class warfare, racism, anxiety, and litigation while enabling lobbyists and politicians to unduly influence our socioeconomic peace. Social engineers use the scheme to further their views of Utopia. The tax policy which was never intended to manipulate social development, has become an avenue for politicians and lobbyists to extend control over all aspects of American life and perpetuate their power grab. People and companies are lured into doing things they would never consider if it were not for the tax scheme. We the people must reinvent this tax scheme if we are to leave a country worth having to our posterity.

Social Security and Medicare will eventually go bankrupt unless the paradigm is changed. The collection of revenue by the Federal government has the same fundamental inadequacies for Income Tax, Social Security, and Medicare. We might as well fix them all at the same time.

Fairness is the inadequacy that screams for action in all three of these improperly implemented schemes. Is double taxation fair? Is massive government intrusion into your personal life fair? Is it fair that many corporations pay no taxes? Is it fair that corporations get tax credits for moving jobs out of the U.S.? Is it fair that renters can not deduct their rent whereas homeowners can claim deductions for as many homes as they may own? Is intimidation by the Internal Revenue Service fair? Is it fair that a person who makes millions of dollars on capital gains pays no Social Security or Medicare? Is the "marriage penalty" fair? Is it fair for a person with 10 children to get preferential tax treatment compared to a person with two children, no children, or single? The fourteenth amendment to the United States Constitution guarantees Americans equal protection from the Federal government.

There is nothing in this book for politicians; this book is for **We the People**. The solutions presented in this volume and subsequent volumes have a common theme in that the solutions are simple to understand, fair to every American, consistent with the Constitution, very doable, budget balancing, create an engine for economic growth, eliminate special interest influences, stop politicians from furthering their personal agendas, forcing politicians to live under the same scheme they impose for other Americans, and the reduction of fraud and corruption.

Many will think this paradigm too radical. Many will like some features and hate other features. The people and organizations that object the most are the ones that have the most to loose in a fair system. Some will say that it can't be that simple. They will be special interests seeing their loopholes close. Some will say it's impossible to implement. To George Washington landing on the moon was impossible. Try to look at this paradigm in its entirety and from the point of view of other Americans. Trade offs were made for fairness and simplicity, the two primary principles driving this anthology. Options are discussed where these trade offs are made so that the rationale for selecting a path is clear.

The great challenge of this book series is presenting a solution that is acceptable to the far left progressive, the far right conservative, and every rational person in between. The progressive insists that the middle class and the poor are protected from the "system" and themselves. The conservative insists on personal responsibility and liberty. The rational person in between insists on compromise. These are not inconsistent purposes.

Chapter 1 - The Best Tax Solution

This book is unlike any other in that the first chapter is the climax and subsequent chapters support the conclusion that this is *The Best Tax Solution* to the revenue ills of the United States. *The Best Tax Solution* is a comprehensive system that addresses all the revenue needs of the United States, including but not limited to income tax, social security, and medicare. *The Best Tax Solution* is best viewed in it's entirety. Any specific characteristic or feature on it's own may be objectionable to one group or another, but taken as a total solution it is *The Best Tax Solution.*

Precisely stated *The Best Tax Solution* is:

<u>A fair and simple income tax for taxpayers.</u>

To be *fair* and *simple* the Internal Revenue Service must be phased out and the 16th Amendment to the United States Constitution should be repealed. The IRS has not been *fair* since the day the 16th Amendment was finally passed on February 3, 1913 with the ratification by Delaware. Class warfare began in earnest on March 15, 1909 when Congress first proposed the 16th Amendment. Implementing *The Best Tax Solution* does not immediately require that the 16th Amendment be repealed or that the IRS be phased out, but they will become superfluous.

The IRS will be replaced by the Income System (**IS**), a highly automated computer system that is impossible to lobby and is dispassionate (*fair*) in determining liability. Most people would never have to file a tax return and would automatically receive the correct refund by the end of February after all their income and payments were tabulated for the prior year. Those having to file would have a *simple* one page tax form, included later in this chapter. With the current tax code this would be virtually impossible, whereas *The Best Tax Solution* makes this not only doable, but understandable to taxpayers and politicians. Imagine a solution where politicians could not deceive the American people and manipulate the tax code for special interests.

Special interests have no place in the Constitutional society Americans have decided to structure their lives around.   The very

Declaration of Independence demands "that all men are created equal". To be *fair*, whether these special interests be corporations, labor unions, or non-profit organizations they are not entitled to special favors that are not available to every other American. Indeed the 14th Amendment to the United States Constitution guarantees every American equal protection under the law. Title 26, the Internal Revenue Title, is nothing more than another law passed through the Constitutional legislative process.

Daniel Webster

The fundamental flaw in the 16th Amendment is it showed total disregard for the Declaration of Independence that stated "that all men are created equal". Even if their intentions were good, they failed to learn the wise words of Constitutional Lawyer, U.S. Senator, and Secretary of State Daniel Webster who said:

*"It is hardly too strong to say that the Constitution was made to guard the people against the dangers of good intentions. There are men in all ages who mean to govern well, but **they mean to govern**. They promise to be good masters, but **they mean to be masters**."*

Politicians became the *elite* when they proposed the 16th Amendment. They had become the *masters* that Daniel Webster warned of when the 16th Amendment was ratified. As *masters* they control Americans by infringing upon liberty and freedom when they require that people divulge how and where their property/money is spent.

Understanding Types of Taxes

Broadly, taxes are of three basic types; progressive, regressive, and proportional. The current tax code is purported to be primarily progressive, but in reality has elements of all three. The 16th Amendment gives Congress the authority to implement a progressive income tax system. Before the 16th Amendment all taxes had to be proportional as stated in Article I Section 8 of the United States Constitution which reads:

"The Congress shall have Power To lay and collect Taxes, Duties, Imposts and Excises, to pay the Debts and provide for the common Defence and general Welfare of the United States; but all Duties, Imposts and Excises shall be uniform throughout the United States;"

Further the 16th Amendment reads:

The Congress shall have power to lay and collect taxes on incomes, from whatever source derived, without apportionment among the several states, and without regard to any census or enumeration.

Clearly the Constitution allows "uniform" proportional taxes on Duties, Imposts, and Excises and a progressive income tax "without regard to any census or enumeration".

Proportional Taxes

Direct taxes are authorized in Article I Section 2 of the Constitution which reads in the relative part; "*... direct taxes shall be apportioned among the several states which may be included within this union, according to their respective numbers...*". Article I Section 9 of the Constitution reads; "*No capitation, or other direct, tax shall be laid, unless in proportion to the census or enumeration herein before directed to be taken.*". In essence the Framers of the Constitution believed that people were to be taxed equally as explained by Albert Gallatin, longest serving Treasurer of the United States, who wrote; "*... by direct taxes in the constitution, those are meant which are raised on the capital or revenue of the people...*". The Framers also followed the writing of Adam Smith who wrote The Wealth of Nations in 1776. A flat tax on income is the prime example of a proportional tax.

Progressive Taxes

Greed motivated the adoption of the 16th Amendment to the Constitution when politicians decided that fairness was overrated, the Framers had it all wrong, they could spend money better than the people, and some people were too wealthy. The first progressive income tax in 1913 ranged from 1% for everyone up to 5% for the very wealthy.

Regressive Taxes

Lower income people are disproportionately impacted by regressive taxes even though they may be applied uniformly, although not exclusively. Regressive taxes come in three varieties; excise, fees, and sales tax. States impose all three types of regressive taxes, whereas the federal government imposes primarily excise tax and fees. Although excise taxes are allowed for in the Constitution, fees by definition are unconstitutional because they are not within the taxing power of the legislative branch as described in Article I of the Constitution. The difference being that excise tax is imposed on commodities and fees are imposed on government services.

Features of The Best Tax Solution

The Best Tax Solution is solely a proportional direct tax. All regressive taxes at the federal level are eliminated. Even though excise taxes are allowed in the Constitution, *The Best Tax Solution* removes the unfair burden they place on the lower income taxpayer.

The Best Tax Solution eliminates special interests by removing **all deductions, credits, and loopholes**. Deductions and loopholes are the method employed by politicians to satisfy their contributors and buy their next election. *The Best Tax Solution* treats all people and corporations as individuals, hence taxpayers. *The Best Tax Solution* stops all forms of double taxation, including death taxes, gifts, tips, and dividends. *The Best Tax Solution* ceases regressive taxes such as gasoline, excise, and surcharges. *The Best Tax Solution* creates parity for hard working taxpayers and strengthens Social Security by shifting the burden completely away from the individual taxpayer to the employer.

The Best Tax Solution creates transparency (what a novel concept) by limiting what can be changed by legislation and politicians. To make it *simple* enough even for politicians to understand, only 4 things can be modified as follows:

1) the subsistence level of $25,000,

2) .the income tax rate of 10%,

3) the Social Security contribution of 5%, and

4) the Medicare/Medicaid (hereinafter referred to as Medicare) contribution of 3%.

Any changes to these 4 parameters are easily understood by the American taxpayer.

Under **no** circumstances does *The Best Tax Solution* permit a scenario where lower income taxpayers pay a higher rate than more wealthy taxpayers. This is true for the babysitter, the hedge fund manager, and the largest multinational corporation. The time of corporations paying no taxes will be over, forever. The days of Warren Buffett paying a lower tax rate than his secretary will be gone, forever.

Barack Hussein Obama

Warren Buffett

Taxes by their very nature are shared sacrifices, as insisted by President Barack Hussein Obama, imposed on taxpayers. Shared sacrifice is only *fair* if everyone has "skin in the game". Warren Buffett coined the phrase "skin in the game" meaning insiders putting their own funds into the venture they're tied to. Are not all Americans insiders tied to the nation's future as individuals and posterity?

Essential Features of The Best Tax Solution

Simplicity is derived by having only four variables that can be modified by legislative action, those being the Subsistence Level, the income tax rate, Social Security contribution rate, and the Medicare contribution rate. Combined income tax, Social Security, and Medicare are hereinafter referred to simply as *taxes*. To assist in preventing fraud, all taxes are withheld on all relative income. *The Best Tax Solution* proposes a starting point for these four variables as follows:

- Subsistence Level of $25,000
- 10% income tax on all income above the subsistence level
- 5% contribution for Social Security on all income
- 3% contribution for Medicare on all income above the subsistence level

This makes *simple* formulas for determining what a taxpayer pays, what an employer pays on behalf of the the taxpayer, and what is withheld on investments. If a taxpayer is not employed by another taxpayer they pay all taxes. That would include self employed people, corporations, partnerships, non-federal governmental entities, non-profit organizations, and any other entity that has income.

The *simple* formula for all taxpayers for income tax and Medicare is:

(income – subsistence level) x (income tax rate + medicare rate)

The *simple* formula for all taxpayers for Social Security is:

income x social security rate

The Social Security portion is paid by employer if income is derived in that manner. If the income is not from an employer or the result of investment, Social Security is paid by the taxpayer.

For example if a taxpayer had $125,000 income from an employer and $100,000 in investment income, taxpayer would have $16,250 ($125,000 x 0.13) withheld by their employer, $18,000 ($100,000 x 0.18) withheld from their investment income, and $6,250 ($125,000 x 0.05) paid by the employer. They would get a refund of $3,250 ($25,000 x 0.13) at the end of the year. The total revenue to the federal government would be $37,250.

Fairness is achieved by applying the 14th Amendment to the United States Constitution which guarantees equal protection. Accordingly, ***The Best Tax Solution*** proposes starting with the following rules:

- All taxpayers are treated as individuals
- All taxpayers get a refund on all withholding paid below the Subsistence Level

To further increase simplicity and fairness there are numerous features of the current federal taxing authority throughout the federal register. ***The Best Tax Solution*** proposes that all statutes and regulations that affect taxpayers wherever they may appear be removed. This means none of the following would exist after implementing ***The Best Tax***

Solution:

- No deductions
- No tax credits
- No tax breaks
- No loopholes
- No double taxation
- No regressive taxes
- No exceptions
- No exemptions
- No extensions

With any societal program there will be entities that do not follow even clear, simple, and fair laws. For those, ***The Best Tax Solution*** includes the following remedies:

- Late charge of 15% for inadequate withholding
- Penalty of 15% for late payment or filing
- Mandatory Criminal penalties for tax cheaters

These features are designed to apply equally to every entity. These entities include an individual, a partnership, a sole proprietorship, a small corporation, a large corporation, a trust fund, a church, a municipality (including states), quasi-government agencies, and foreign concerns involved in United States commerce.

The reason these features are essential in addition to fairness and simplicity include transparency and limits on government power. The more variables allowed to Congress increases possibilities of special interest influence. By limiting Congress to four variables, true transparency is achieved and Congress can spend their time reducing spending and fixing more urgent problems. How easy would it be to evaluate a candidate if their position on these four variables were known?

Each of these features are discussed in more detail in later chapters where the rationale of the feature is explained in conjunction with the purpose of ***The Best Tax Solution.*** Unlike tax schemes proposed by others, *The Best Tax Solution* is limited to these features, there are no more.

Characteristics of The Best Tax Solution

Other desirable consequences of *The Best Tax Solution* will manifest themselves when **fair** and **simple** are implemented. An analysis of this statement requires a concise definition of the words; fair, simple, income, tax, and taxpayers.

By definition of the word *fair*, the current tax system is not *fair* because every year changes are made that would indicate that last year was not *fair* or this year is not *fair*. Since 1986, when the last attempt was made to implement a *fair* tax system, the scheme has been found to be unfair over 14,000 times. *The Best Tax Solution* uses the 14th Amendment of the United States Constitution to help define *fair*.

By definition of the word *simple*, the current tax system is not *simple* because everyone is responsible for following 80,000 pages of IRS statutes, rules, and regulations when more than half the time IRS does not understand them. Even persons responsible for enforcing the tax system, former Treasury Secretary Timothy Geitner, and the person responsible for creating the tax system, the prior Chairman of the House Ways and Means Committee Charles Rangel can not and/or did not follow the tax law. *The Best Tax Solution* defines *simple* so that even government officials can understand their obligations.

The definition of the word *income* in the current tax system IRS throws out terms such as earned income, unearned income, gross income, adjusted gross income, dividends, interest, retained earnings, and capital gains, to name a few. *The Best Tax Solution* defines *income* one way and one way only; revenue that has not yet been taxed. For now to keep it simple, an individual's revenue is any money or increase in net worth that accrues to a person's benefit and a corporation's revenue is gross sales less cost of goods sold, less cost of sales, and less dividends paid. There is an entire chapter devoted to explaining *income* because people tend to manufacture their own definition to help justify their self-serving intentions.

The definition of the word *tax* is a confiscatory procedure that governments use to accumulate wealth that they believe they can spend better than the taxpayer. ***The Best Tax Solution*** defines ***tax*** as a payment from taxpayers in order to implement a power of the United States government as described in the United States Constitution.

The definition of the word ***taxpayer*** in the current tax system is any entity (individual or company) that the government relieves of perceived excessive net worth or any entity (individual or company) that the government believes that it's entitled to other people's money. ***The Best Tax Solution*** defines ***taxpayer*** as any and every entity that has income in the United States of America and/or it's territories plus any income worldwide from U.S. Citizens, permanent residents, corporations headquartered in the United States, and foreign individuals and corporations doing business in the United States. ***The Best Tax Solution*** treats them all the same.

What is Fair?

Fair can be an adjective, adverb, or noun. For the purpose of describing a fair tax system, the adjective is the most appropriate and is defined by the Free Merriam-Webster Online Dictionary.

Is it ***fair*** that:
1. married couples pay more than if they were individuals?
2. people with 10 children are subsidized by everyone else?
3. each and every taxpayer is treated differently?
4. multi-billion dollar corporations pay no taxes?
5. tax deductions are given to corporations to move jobs offshore or to close plants?
6. everyone is responsible for following 80,000 pages of IRS statutes, rules, and regulations when more than half the time IRS does not understand them?
7. hundreds of billions of dollars are spent and billions of hours are wasted each year to comply with the IRS?
8. persons at the poverty level pay a higher percentage of their pay to the government than the millionaire investor?
9. there is double taxation on estates, gifts, and dividends?
10. politicians and lobbyists blatantly manipulate the tax code to further their own goals?

There are hundreds, if not tens of thousands, of aspects of the current tax system that are not fair. Entire books could and have been written on the subject. Suffice it to say that the current tax system is not fair. To really solve this dilemma and create an income tax system that is truly fair an unambiguous definition of fair is essential.

The Best Tax Solution uses a definition consistent with the 14th Amendment of the United States Constitution guaranteeing equal protection. *The Best Tax Solution* definition of *fair* from the Free Merriam-Webster Online Dictionary is *marked by impartiality and honesty : free from self-interest, prejudice, or favoritism.*

According to the definition of *fair* used by *The Best Tax Solution* all 10 of the items listed above are <u>not</u> *fair*. How can anyone be expected to pay their *fair* share when the tax code itself is not *fair*? People of all ideologies believe in everyone paying their *fair* share, but they can not seem to agree on what is *fair* because the system is so unfair. Making the tax code *fair* will by necessity define what *fair* share really looks like.

What is Simple?

Simple can be an adjective or noun. For the purpose of describing a *simple* tax system, the adjective is the most appropriate and is defined by the Free Merriam-Webster Online Dictionary.

Is it *simple* when:
1. tax returns are like snowflakes (no two being the same)?
2. the average taxpayer spends hundreds of hours trying to comply?
3. there are thousands of new pages in the tax code every year?
4. the IRS gets it wrong more often than not?
5. billions of hours are wasted avoiding paying taxes?
6. the former Treasury Secretary can't correctly file a tax return?
7. the prior Chairman of the Ways and Means committee in Congress (Charlie Rangel) doesn't know the laws that he helped pass?
8. a brain or heart surgeon can't complete a tax return

without help?
9. 3 million people are needed to manage and administer the system?
10. ten CPAs prepare the same tax return and get ten different results?

Suffice it to say that the current tax code is not *simple*. To really solve this dilemma and create an income tax system that is truly *simple,* an unambiguous definition of *simple* is imperative.

The Best Tax Solution uses a definition consistent with what the average person believes. ***The Best Tax Solution*** definition of *simple* from the Free Merriam-Webster Online Dictionary is *readily understood or performed.*

According to the definition of *simple* used by ***The Best Tax Solution*** all 10 of the items listed above are <u>not</u> *simple*. *Simple* means a tax return prepared by a literate gas station attendant will be the same as a large corporation. Not that the results will be the same, but the ease of compliance must be simple enough to eliminate the need for third-party preparers for virtually all taxpayers. The billions of hours and dollars spent in compliance with the overly complex tax code is better used on more productive and fun pursuits.

What is Income?

Income is a noun. For the purpose of describing a *income* tax system, the most appropriate is defined by the Free Merriam-Webster Online Dictionary.

Is it *income* when:
1. a child gets an allowance or money from the tooth fairy?
2. a kid opens a lemonade stand or delivers newspapers?
3. a waitress or taxicab driver receives a tip for good service?
4. a person inherits money?
5. a woman receives alimony and/or child support?
6. a retiree receives pension benefits or social security?
7. a person receives money in a lawsuit settlement?
8. an employee receives healthcare benefits?

9. a person sells a used car or house?
10. an executive receives stock options?

Income is the most nebulous definition used in ***The Best Tax Solution***. An entire chapter is devoted to it, so that executives can be clear what their responsibilities are concerning *income*.

The Best Tax Solution uses a definition consistent with what the average person believes. ***The Best Tax Solution*** definition of *income* from the Free Merriam-Webster Online Dictionary is *a gain or recurrent benefit usually measured in money that derives from capital or labor; also : the amount of such gain received in a period of time.*

According to the definition of *income* used by ***The Best Tax Solution*** only 3 of the items listed above are *income*. The current tax code considers at least 7 of the items as *income*.

What is a Tax?

Tax can be a transitive verb or a noun. For the purpose of describing a *tax*, the most appropriate is the noun defined by the Free Merriam-Webster Online Dictionary.

Is it a *tax* when:
1. the government says it is a fine or a penalty?
2. the government calls it a fee?
3. there is a tariff on imported goods?
4. it is called an assessment?
5. it is called Social Security or Medicare?
6. it is called unemployment or disability insurance?
7. it is called a surcharge?
8. it is called excise?
9. it is on gasoline?
10. it is a duty on imports?

Tax is the most obvious definition used in ***The Best Tax Solution***.

The Best Tax Solution uses a definition consistent with what the average person believes. ***The Best Tax Solution*** definition of *tax* from the Free Merriam-Webster Online Dictionary is *a charge usually of money imposed by authority on persons or property for public purposes*

According to the definition of tax used by ***The Best Tax Solution*** all of the items listed are ***tax***. Keeping in mind that many of these items are also imposed by state or local governments and this volume only deals with federal revenues. For example the Supreme Court has ruled that Obamacare is a ***tax***, irrespective of the definition used in ***The Best Tax Solution.*** The current IRS tax code considers only the fine imposed by Obamacare as ***tax***.

Who is a Taxpayer?

Taxpayer is a noun. For the purpose of describing a ***taxpayer***, the most appropriate is defined by the Free Merriam-Webster Online Dictionary.

Is someone a ***taxpayer*** when:
1. they have federal tax withheld from their paycheck?
2. they pay federal gasoline tax?
3. they have Social Security withheld from their paycheck?
4. they have Medicare withheld from their paycheck?
5. they pay capital gains or dividend tax?
6. they get an earned income credit?
7. they pay tax on their assets when they die?
8. they pay a passport fee?
9. they pay telephone surcharges?
10. they pay an airport security fee?

Taxpayer is the most unambiguous definition used in ***The Best Tax Solution***.

The Best Tax Solution uses a definition consistent with what the average person believes. ***The Best Tax Solution*** definition of ***taxpayer*** from the Free Merriam-Webster Online Dictionary is *one that pays or is liable for a tax*

According to the definition of taxpayer used by ***The Best Tax Solution*** all of the entities listed above are ***taxpayers***. The current IRS tax code considers only 6 of them as *taxpayers*.

Franklin Roosevelt

Charles Ponzi

The Best Tax Solution does not care whether the Social Security Act of 1935, a product of the New Deal by Franklin D. Roosevelt, is Constitutional or a Ponzi scheme. To call Social Security a Ponzi scheme is disingenuous at best and inflammatory at worst. Jonathan Bernstein[1] wrote "anyone who says that Social Security is a Ponzi scheme either misunderstands Social Security, misunderstands Ponzi schemes, is deliberately lying, or some combination of those." Social Security is a Ponzi scheme only if it's used as a metaphor, and not a very good one at that. Social Security is a social safety net designed to ensure that all Americans can survive with dignity in the twilight of their lives. Whether you agree with it or not, it's institutionalized until something better comes along.

Both political parties Democrats and Republicans use Social Security to demonize the other party. The Democrats try to scare old people into believing the Republicans want to take away their Social Security, and Republicans try to scare everyone else by stating Social Security is going bankrupt. For anybody that believes the rhetoric by either party, there is a bridge in Brooklyn for sale that's on the market for less than $1,000. ***The Best Tax Solution*** only deals with securing the revenue component of the system **forever**, or until something better comes along.

The Best Tax Solution treats Social Security as a defined benefit plan and by that definition it is funded **only** by the employer. For simplicity sake, the difference between a defined benefit (DB) plan and a defined contribution (DC or 401K) plan is that the DB plan **indirectly** equates to the dollars and/or hours that you and your employer contribute

---

1 *Jonathan Bernstein is a political scientist who writes about American politics for the Washington Post, Salon, and The American Prospect.*

to the plan and the DC plan **<u>directly</u>** equates to the dollars you and/or your employer contribute to the plan. What is the point of having a safety net for all Americans that is directly tied to an individual?   Anyone, mainly Republicans, that think Social Security should be privatized and turned into a DC plan is missing the purpose and intent of this social safety net.

Certainly some changes must be made in Social Security, the first should be how contributions are collected. *The Best Tax Solution* puts the funding, where it belongs, on the employer, self-employed person, and companies. *The Best Tax Solution* institutes a 5% contribution, with no upper limit, by any employer, self-employed person, or company. If an employee has a income of $100,000 the employer pays $5,000. If a self-employed person has income of $1,000,000 they pay $50,000. If a company has income of $1,000,000,000 they pay $50,000,000. Everyone pays their fair share.

Why would *The Best Tax Solution* have companies contribute to Social Security? Look at the purpose of Social Security, it's a social safety net for all Americans. The Supreme Court has decided in its "infinite" wisdom, that companies enjoy many of the same constitutional rights as other people, so why shouldn't they contribute to the social guarantee?

What's good for the goose is good for the gander.

Medicare/Medicaid

The Best Tax Solution does not care whether the Social Security Amendments of 1965, a product of the Great Society by Lyndon B. Johnson, is Constitutional. Medicare/Medicaid, hereinafter referred to as Medicare, is a social safety net health insurance designed to ensure that all Americans can survive with dignity in the twilight of their lives and impoverished Americans can obtain healthcare. Whether you agree with it or not, it's reality until something better comes along.

Lyndon Johnson at Great Society Speech

Unlike Social Security, Medicare is not even indirectly tied to an individual. In essence the program is a forced charitable contribution. That is why ***The Best Tax Solution*** treats it that way. If individuals are forced to make a charitable contribution, why should companies be given a free ride?

Both political parties Democrats and Republicans use Medicare to demonize the other party. The Democrats try to scare old people and poor people into believing the Republicans want to take away their Medicare, and Republicans try to scare everyone else by stating Medicare is going bankrupt. For anybody that believes the rhetoric by either party, there is a bridge in San Francisco for sale that's on the market for less than $1,000. ***The Best Tax Solution*** only deals with securing the revenue component of the system **forever**, or until something better comes along.

Certainly some changes must be made in Medicare, the first should be how contributions are collected. ***The Best Tax Solution*** puts the funding, where it belongs, on the individual receiving income whatever type of entity it might be. ***The Best Tax Solution*** institutes a 3% contribution (above the subsistence level), with no upper limit, by any entity. If an employee has a income of $100,000 the employee pays

$2,250 (($100,000 - $25,000) x 0.03). If a self-employed person has income of $1,000,000 they pay $29,250 (($1,000,000 - $25,000) x 0.03). If a company has income of $1,000,000,000 they pay $29,999,250. Everyone pays their fair share.

A fundamental problem with Medicare and Medicaid is the lack of delineation. While the Federal government administers Medicare, the states administer Medicaid with micromanagement from the Federal government. Since Medicare charges premiums when actually used and premiums are means tested, the withholding is the sole revenue provider for Medicaid!! Why should states pay the Federal government the 40% overhead on Medicaid if the states are required to administer the program? Alas, that is a topic for Volume II.

The Best Tax Solution in Action

Implementing **The Best Tax Solution** is explained in detail in Chapter 6. **The Best Tax Solution** will be known as the Income System (*IS*), a bureau of the Treasury Department. *IS* utilizes a sophisticated integrated platform using personal computers, smart phones, corporate networks, financial institutions, third-party administrators, government agencies, and the Internet. Security is maintained by using SSL[1] and PKI[2] certificates, multi-factor authentication, and certified mail. All taxpayers will pay income tax, Social Security, and Medicare. There will be no deductions or credits of any kind irrespective of the taxpayer's situation. There will be no double taxation. There will be no tax of any kind on gifts. There will be no income exempt from taxation. There will be no death tax on assets that have already been taxed. Assets that have not been taxed (i.e. 401K balances) will be taxed upon death.

Revenue flows to the federal government through withholding, periodic payments, and penalties. Every financial institution will have a federal government account that accepts deposits. Deposits can be made in a variety of ways, including in person, through ATM[3], as ACH[4] transactions, or wire transfers (wire transfers may be subject to fees). Returned deposits may be subject to fees by the financial institution and

---

1   Secure Sockets Layer
2   Public Key Infrastructure
3   Automated Teller Machine
4   Automated Clearing House

will incur a 15% penalty that must be submitted with any subsequent deposit. Revenue is returned to the taxpayer through refunds. The vast majority of taxpayers will interact with *IS* electronically.

All taxpayers will maintain an online taxpayer profile that includes their name, physical address, an email address, Social Security number or taxpayer identification number, a cell phone, a bank account with routing number and account number, and various authentication answers.

Withholding

All transactions that result in income are subject to withholding. This includes, but is not limited to, wages from employers, dividends on investments, interest on investments, and gains from sales of assets. The federal government will withhold from Social Security benefits above the subsistence level. Withholding is due when the transaction occurs. An employer pays the withholding when the employee is paid. A company that pays dividends withholds when the dividend is paid. A borrower pays withholding when making interest payments on debt, including to or from the government. Failure to properly withhold is subject to a 15% penalty on the amount due.

Withholding is not practical for companies that sell numerous products and/or services. Companies will be required to pay taxes on no longer than a monthly basis on their operating income. Companies are still required to pay taxes on their investment income at the time the income is realized. Their withholding on employees paychecks is due the same day that employees are paid.

Periodic Payments

Companies must pay taxes weekly if they are on a cash basis and monthly if they are on an accrual basis. Taxes must be paid within five business days of the end of the period. These periodic tax payments will be estimates and can be reconciled at the end of the year on the income statement. If companies pay their taxes late, they will be subject to a 15% penalty. At the end of the year, if they have paid insufficient taxes there will be another 15% penalty on the shortage.

Taxpayer Profile

Every taxpayer must establish an online profile that may be maintained by smartphone, personal computer, and/or by certified mail. The minimal information will include the taxpayer name, physical address, an email address, Social Security number or taxpayer identification number, and various authentication answers. Optionally, taxpayers may supply a cell phone and a bank account with routing number and account number. Taxpayers domiciled outside the United States and territories are not exempted from these requirements and must maintain their profile information electronically.

Income Statement

Every taxpayer is entitled to file an income statement, although it is not necessary for most taxpayers. The statement may be filed by U.S. mail or electronically.

Taxpayers required to file an income statement are 1) any entity that has a cost-of-goods and/or a cost-of-sales, 2) any first time taxpayer, and 3) any taxpayer reporting a name change, address change, or bank account change. If a taxpayer is a first time taxpayer or is only reporting information change, they may file the form at any time without showing income. For those that do not file an income statement and none is required, they will receive an income statement with their refund.

When possible, income statements will be filed electronically, emailed to the taxpayer, and refunds will be direct deposited. Non-electronic filing will result in delayed refunds. For those that do not file and are due a refund, the income statement will be emailed by February 15th and the refund made at the same time.

INCOME STATEMENT
UNITED STATES INCOME SYSTEM
RETURN OF ANNUAL INCOME

INCOME RECEIVED DURING THE YEAR ENDING ________________, 20______.

Filed for ________________________________ Tax ID ________________

of

____
(Street Number, Street Name, Apartment Number, City, County, State, Zip/Postal Code, Country)

---

1. *Income Received* .... $_____,_____,_____,_____,_____
2. *Subsistence Level* .... $ 2 5 , 0 0 0
3. *Taxable Income (line 1 - line 2, if more than 0)* $_____,_____,_____,_____,_____
4. *Income Tax Owed (10% of line 3)* .... $_____,_____,_____,_____,_____
5. *Medicare Owed (3% of line 3)* .... $_____,_____,_____,_____,_____
6. *Social Security Owed (5% of line 1)* .... $_____,_____,_____,_____,_____
7. *Social Security Paid by Employer(s)* .... $_____,_____,_____,_____,_____
8. *Income Tax, Social Security, and Medicare Owed*
   (add lines 4 through 6 and subtract line 7) ...... $_____,_____,_____,_____,_____
9. *Income Tax, Social Security, & Medicare Paid* . $_____,_____,_____,_____,_____
10. *Income Tax, Social Security, and Medicare Due*
   (line 8 minus line 9, if more than 0) .... $_____,_____,_____,_____,_____
11. *Under Payment Penalty (15% of line 10)* .... $_____,_____,_____,_____,_____
12. *Total Due to IS (add lines 10 and 11)* .... $_____,_____,_____,_____,_____
13. *Refund Due (line 9 minus line 8, if more than 0)* $_____,_____,_____,_____,_____

Routing Number ______________ Account Number ______________

Sworn, under penalty of perjury, on this ______ day of ________________,________
                                        (Day)   (Month)   (Year)

by____
(Signature and Title)

Prepared by (if not taxpayer) ________________ Tax Id ______________

Instructions for Completing Income Statement

Year Ending:
For all individuals and most companies this is a calendar year ending on December 31. For those companies that are on a fiscal year other than a calendar year, it is the last day of a month. To avoid an audit this date must be the last day of a month and match the year ending date on the previous year income statement, if applicable.

Filed for:
This is the name of the taxpayer on the last day of the year. To avoid an audit it must match exactly the name on the online taxpayer profile.

Tax ID:
For individuals this is a Social Security number. For all other entities this is a Taxpayer Identification Number. To avoid an audit it must match exactly the Tax ID on the online taxpayer profile.

of:
This is a physical address that must include where applicable a Street Number, Street Name, Apartment Number, City, County, State or Province, Zip/Postal Code, and Country. Post office boxes are not acceptable. To avoid an audit it must match exactly the address on the online taxpayer profile.

Line 1   Income Received:
A gain or recurrent benefit usually measured in money that derives from capital or labor; also : the amount of such gain received in a period of time. A detailed definition can be found in IS Publication 1 (Included in this book as Chapter 2 – Income).

Line 2   Subsistence Level:
This amount of $25,000 is allowed to all taxpayers before they start paying income tax and Medicare.

Line 3   Taxable Income:
This amount is the Income Received from Line 1 less the Subsistence level

of Line 2. If it is less than zero, enter 0.

Line 4   Income Tax Owed:
This amount is 10% of Taxable Income from Line 3.

Line 5   Medicare Owed:
This amount is 3% of Taxable Income from Line 3.

Line 6   Social Security Owed:
This amount is 5% of Income Received from Line 1. If Line 1 is in any part derived from Social Security benefits, enter 0.

Line 7   Social Security Paid by Employer(s):
This amount is the total paid by all employers or withheld from any income source during the year. The last pay stub from each employer will show the amount they paid for Social Security on your behalf and investment statements will include the amount withheld.

Line 8   Income Tax, Social Security, and Medicare Owed:
This amount is Income Tax Owed from Line 4; plus Medicare Owed from Line 5; plus Social Security Owed from Line 6; minus Social Security Paid by Employer(s) from Line 7.

Line 9   Income Tax, Social Security, and Medicare Paid:
This amount is the total Income Tax and Medicare withheld by all employers and investments; plus periodic payments for Income Tax, Medicare, and Social Security made by taxpayer; plus Income Tax, Medicare, and Social Security withheld from investment income.

Line 10   Income Tax, Social Security, and Medicare Due:
This amount is Income Tax, Social Security, and Medicare Owed from Line 8; minus Income Tax, Social Security, and Medicare Paid from Line 9. If less than zero, enter 0.

Line 11   Under Payment Penalty (15% of line 10):
If Income Tax, Social Security, and Medicare Due from Line 10 is greater than zero, enter 15% of Line 10, otherwise enter 0.

Line 12   Total Due to IS:
If Income Tax, Social Security, and Medicare Due from Line 10 is greater than zero, add Lines 10 and Line 11.

Line 13   Refund Due:
If Income Tax, Social Security, and Medicare Paid from Line 8 is greater than Income Tax, Social Security, and Medicare Owed from Line 9 is greater than zero, then enter Line 9 minus minus Line 8, otherwise enter 0.
If greater than zero enter a Routing Number and Account Number where the refund will be deposited. To avoid an audit this must match the Routing Number and Account Number in the taxpayer profile.

Date and sign the Income Statement. If signing for a company print name of signer and title. If Income Statement was prepared by a third-party, enter the name, signature, and Tax ID of the preparer.

Chapter 2 - Income

Income comes in many forms, but *The Best Tax Solution* uses a concise definition that can be applied without ambiguity to any transaction. Specifically, *The Best Tax Solution* defines income as: *a gain or recurrent benefit usually measured in money that derives from capital or labor.* Remember, No Double Taxation, No Deductions, and No Exceptions.

When a child gets an allowance or money from the tooth fairy it is not income because there is no capital or labor involved. Only the most cynical person would contend that a tooth is capital or that an allowance is given because of labor. In spite of allowances being given for good grades or completion of chores it is not a requirement of either and can more closely be considered a gift. The current tax system does not consider this income nor does *The Best Tax Solution.* No double taxation.

When a kid opens a lemonade stand or delivers newspapers it is income because labor is involved. For a lemonade stand capital is also required, even though the capital is usually given as a gift from parents. Delivering papers, in addition to other services such as babysitting, is income because it is all labor. The current tax system does not classify this labor as income and requires no withholding, social security, or medicare. *The Best Tax Solution* treats any transaction involving labor as income, regardless of the age or type of labor. No exceptions.

When a waitress or taxicab driver receives a tip for good service it is not income because first of all it is not required and secondly it has already been taxed. Gifts by definition are not taxable because they are not derived from capital and are not mandatory. There are exceptions, like a restaurant that requires a gratuity for parties of six or more. In that case it is income because it is mandatory, like it or not. The current tax system classifies this as income, whereas *The Best Tax Solution* does not consider this as income because there is no capital involved, the labor does not necessarily require the gratuity, and the money has already been taxed. No double taxation.

When a person inherits money or assets it is not income. It's questionable whether it is even Constitutional to tax inheritances, because it's property. Nowhere does the Constitution allow seizure of property without due process. Although it may be capital, it is not derived from capital or from labor. Besides, the estate of the deceased person may be liable for income in the current year. The deceased person may also be due a refund for the current year, but not for any capital or assets on which they have already paid taxes. The current tax system has elaborate thresholds for calculating inheritance taxes. *The Best Tax Solution* considers this transaction a gift to the recipient and not income. The deceased person is only responsible for the transactions that occurred in the year of their death. <u>No double taxation.</u>

When a spouse receives alimony and/or child support it is not income. The funds have already been taxed. Since there would be no deduction, the spouse would have already paid taxes. Divorce settlements should not be determined because of tax consequences. Other people should not be made to pay for another person's selection in marriage or separation. The transaction is treated as a gift to the aggrieved spouse and/or the children. Taxpayers must accept responsibility and face the consequences of their behavior and decisions. The current tax system allows the deduction of alimony to the payer and treats the payments as unearned income to the recipient, and child support is not deductible for the payer or the recipient. IRS has dozens of pages describing the repercussions from divorces and QDROs (Qualified Domestic Relation Orders). *The Best Tax Solution* considers these transactions a gift to the recipient and not income. It is none of the federal government's business to reward or penalize any person for their marital choices. <u>No double taxation. No exceptions.</u>

When a retiree receives pension benefits or social security it is income if it has not previously been taxed. Why should persons without pensions and/or minimal social security subsidize other people that were more fortunate to have lucrative pension income and/or above average social security income? The current tax system treats pensions as taxable and social security above an arbitrary threshold. The IRS excludes various special interest groups from their rules and does not collect medicare or social security on these incomes to the detriment of other taxpayers. ***The Best Tax Solution*** treats any transaction involving labor as income, regardless of when the income is received. <u>No double taxation. No exceptions.</u>

When a person receives money in a lawsuit settlement for damages it is not income, except to the attorneys. First, the awarder can not deduct the reward and the awardee funds are not derived from capital or from labor, in most cases. If the award is for unpaid labor or revenue from capital it is a type of actual damages. In cases where actual damages are considered income to the awardee, they may also be costs to the awarder. In simple language, the current tax system categorizes awards into actual damages, compensatory damages, and punitive damages. For the most part, IRS treats compensatory and punitive damages as income to the awardee, but allows the awarder to write-off the award. ***The Best Tax Solution*** only taxes the awardee for the portion of the income that is derived from labor or capital, and does not allow the awarder a write-off. The attorneys from both sides pay taxes on their income. <u>No double taxation. No deductions. No exceptions.</u>

When an employee receives healthcare benefits it is income. The benefit is derived from labor, regardless of whether the person is currently working or a retiree. Is it right that people without this benefit from their employer or those that pay their own healthcare have to subsidize the more fortunate of those that receive hundreds if not thousands in this benefit? The current tax systems treats this as a deduction for the employer and not income for the employee. ***The Best Tax Solution*** only taxes the employee who receives the benefit. The employer rolls this expense into their cost of labor, if it is also part of their cost of operations. <u>No exceptions. No deductions.</u>

When a person sells a used car or house it is only income for the portion that is in excess of the cost of the asset. This applies to any asset, including commodities, stocks, and widgets. Assets are derived from capital. This sale of assets applies to all assets, from the sale of a bicycle to the sale of a corporation. The current tax system picks winners and losers by exempting some assets, ignoring others, and allowing deductions for others. Some of those ignored are rare coin trading, online sales, charitable sales of donated gifts, and a plethora of miscellaneous items. ***The Best Tax Solution*** only taxes the items where the increase in principal is not the result of a gift. <u>No double taxation.</u>

When an executive receives stock options it is income at the time the options become vested. The options are derived from their labor from the time the options are granted until such time the options are vested, the income being the difference between the value of the stock options when granted and the value of the stock options when vested. The current tax system treats these as income only when the stock options are exercised. The IRS's, and the financial system in general, handling of stock options favors the person receiving the options to the detriment of other taxpayers. ***The Best Tax Solution*** taxes the options when they become vested, and then again when they are exercised. <u>No exceptions.</u>

Income looks differently for individuals, companies, non profit entities, and governments. For purposes of ***The Best Tax Solution***, companies can be any type of corporation, partnership, or joint venture formed with the intention of making a profit. Non profit entities include churches, charities, associations, labor unions, and numerous private organizations. Government entities that generate income include golf courses, transportation systems, stadiums, mail delivery, and student loans; specifically anything that government does that is in competition with the private sector. What makes governments think they have the right to avoid paying taxes for things the private sector would be paying taxes? <u>No exceptions.</u>

Individuals

An individual receives income for performing labor via various methods such as salary, commission, hourly, per task, bonuses, benefits, stock options, exchange of services or combination of these methods. Keep in mind that *The Best Tax Solution* defines income to an individual as any money or increase in net worth that accrues to a person's benefit <u>No exceptions.</u>

Pre-Entry Level and Interns

Many young people earn spending money by performing various tasks such as babysitting, delivering newspapers, mowing lawns, and walking dogs to name a few. They are usually paid on a task or hourly basis. Currently most of this labor is not reported by the person performing the labor or the person paying for the labor. Most of these tasks provide young people with valuable experience, discipline, as well as some walking around money. When these people are paid, *The Best Tax Solution* considers it income. <u>No exceptions.</u>

Interns perform services for little or no pay to ostensibly gain experience or ingratiate themselves for a future job opportunity. The intern is receiving value, as is the employer. Currently the labor is not reported because no money is paid. Internship is a form of barter where each party derives benefit. *The Best Tax Solution* treats interns as unpaid minimum wage employees. Since the intern is performing labor, the employer is obligated to pay the social security contribution as if the intern were earning minimum wage (currently $7.25 per hour making contribution about 36 cents per hour worked) and the intern is obligated to pay the income tax and medicare (about 94 cents per hour worked – most of which will be refunded if the intern has no other income). <u>No exceptions.</u>

Employee

An employee is where a majority of working people are identified. The vast majority being hourly or salaried employees. Employees can be full time, part time, seasonal, or even work a single project. Employee income includes their wages and all benefits. These benefits may include any combination of healthcare, pension, 401K, paid vacations, paid sick-leave, performance bonuses, stock options, and other things of value such as an automobile, cell phone, paid tuition, etc. All of these benefits have a value and that value is income. <u>No exceptions.</u>

Lawyer

Most lawyers are employees of corporations, partnerships, or governmental agencies and ***The Best Tax Solution*** treats them as any other employee. For those that do business as a sole proprietorship all revenue they receive for services rendered and expenses is income. This includes any monies they may receive as a retainer that are not deposited to an escrow trust account whose interest is paid to the bar association. When an attorney takes money from an escrow trust account for services rendered it immediately becomes income. <u>No exceptions.</u>

Independent Consultant

An independent consultant is usually a highly skilled professional working either through an agency or directly for a company that does not want a full time employee or can not find an employee within their required time-frame. The consultant may charge by the hour or a fixed price for a specific task or project. If the consultant works directly for a company, then all revenue from the company is income including reimbursed expenses. If the consultant works through an agency, then all revenue from the agency is income including reimbursed expenses. The amount the agency keeps is their income. <u>No exceptions.</u>

Investor

An investor can apply to anyone who uses the return on capital as revenue. This applies to United States citizens, permanent residents, and foreign nationals. For U.S. citizens and permanent residents, all worldwide income from investments is counted. For foreign nationals income is only taxed for investments made in the United States, including the stock, commodity, or bond markets. Investors may invest in stocks, bonds, commodities, companies, or widgets. Investments can return periodic dividends which are income. At the point an investment reaches fruition, the difference between the initial investment and the return is income (currently capital gains). Any expenses making or disposing of an investment is not deductible. Each transaction regardless of size is evaluated on its own merit. If it makes money it is income. If it does not make money, it is a shame. A shame does not offset income. <u>No deductions. No exceptions.</u>

For Profit Companies

Income to corporations can be derived from operations or investments. Income from investments of corporations is treated exactly the same as if they were an individual investor. ***The Best Tax Solution*** defines income from operations as the difference between revenue less cost-of-goods (COGS) less cost-of-sales (COS) less <u>dividends</u> (unlike the IRS). COGS, COS, and dividends are the cost of doing business and are not deductions. <u>No double taxation.</u>

A company can be either a service provider, a manufacturer, a retailer or any combination of the three. For example, a restaurant could qualify as all three; they may manufacture meals from raw ingredients, they may sell prepackaged food or other items from suppliers, and they may present them to customers. A total service based company derives all of their income from performing work for other people, companies, or government. Whereas, a manufacturer builds widgets[2] from raw materials and a retailer (a "wholesaler" is a type of retailer) sells widgets or services provided by others. Widgets and services are collectively referred to as **products**, hereinafter.

Manufacturing Simply Explained

Simply stated manufacturing is a repetitive process, generally using machines, that makes a product, called finished goods, from raw materials, components, and assemblies. In the simplest terms there may be many things needed for manufacturing, including 1) raw materials, 2) components, 3) assemblies, 4) finished goods, 5) labor, 6) facilities, and 7) machines.

1. Raw materials are unprocessed or minimally processed materials used to make a product. Raw materials are incorporated into a product or consumed in the creation of a product. Energy consumed in the process can be considered a raw material. One company's minimally processed product may be a raw material for another company. For example, lumber may be used to provide energy for the manufacturing process.

---

2   Widgets can be any item from an automobile, dress, airplane, doughnut; essentially any noun that can be sold

2. Components are products that are used in the construction of a more complicated product. For example, a memory chip is a component to a smart phone.
3. Assemblies are products composed of raw materials and components for use in more complex products. For example an alternator is an assembly used in building a car.
4. Finished goods are the final result of the manufacturing process. Finished goods may be composed of raw materials, components, and assemblies. For example an airplane. A finished good for one company may be a raw material, a component, or assembly for another company.
5. Labor is used to build products. Labor is usually human, but can be animal. Manufacturing may not use labor directly in the process, but labor is necessary to maintain machines and/or robots.
6. Facilities are the space required to build products. Examples would be a lab or a building.
7. Machines are used to increase productivity in the manufacturing process. Without machines and robots many manufacturing processes would not be possible.

The Best Tax Solution treats items directly involved in the manufacturing process as cost-of-goods. Items not directly tied to the manufacturing process, i.e. corporate headquarters, management above line managers, machines for packaging finished goods, facilities storing inventory, and shipping docks for receiving materials are not a cost-of-goods. Only portions of facilities and machines contained in the assembly line are cost-of-goods, all others are overhead in the manufacturing process.

Cost -of-Goods (COGS)

The Best Tax Solution determines the COGS for products manufactured in the United States, identically for companies headquartered in the United States and foreign companies. The COGS for companies manufacturing in the United States includes all the labor, raw materials, components, assemblies, energy, actual facilities, and actual machines used in the production of a product, irrespective of the source. Only facilities and machines used in the assembly line are part of

COGS. Since there is no depreciation with *The Best Tax Solution* only actual rent or capital paid for plant and equipment are allowed as COGS. Under no circumstances is overhead including accounting, legal, interest, or management considered as a COGS. No exceptions.

The Best Tax Solution considers COGS for products manufactured internationally and sold in the United States, as only the following: 1) cost of raw materials required to make a product, 2) cost of labor in the United States to make the product, 3) cost of energy in the United States to make the product, and 4) cost of United States content used to make the product. Anything not listed here is not considered a COGS. *The Best Tax Solution* does not consider any of the following as COGS for products sold in the United States and manufactured outside the United States: 1) shipping, 2) research and development (R&D), 3) infrastructure including buildings and equipment, 4) upper management, 5) general administrative overhead including accounting and legal, 6) foreign labor for finished goods without United States content, 7) transaction fees by facilitators (i.e. banks and credit cards), 8) duties and tariffs on imports, and 9) interest on advances and loans. No exceptions.

The Best Tax Solution considers COGS for products manufactured internationally and sold internationally is applicable only to United States headquartered companies. Foreign companies manufacturing internationally and selling internationally have no obligation to the United States. The COGS for United States companies manufacturing internationally and selling internationally includes all the labor, raw materials, components, assemblies, and energy used in the production of a product. Under no circumstances is overhead including accounting and legal considered as a COGS.

The only COGS for a total service based company doing business in the United States is labor performed in the United States. Out-sourced labor for foreign labor is not considered a COGS by *The Best Tax Solution*. No exceptions.

COGS for a retailer selling in the United States is the cost of the finished goods produced in the United States, plus the cost of raw materials irrespective of the source, plus the cost of content in finished goods produced in the United States. <u>No exceptions.</u>

Shipping under no circumstances can be considered a component of COGS. <u>No exceptions.</u>

Restaurants

A restaurant could have COGS comprising of food, energy for cooking and cooling, electricity for lighting, water for serving and cleaning, and labor for chefs, waiters, busboys, and dishwashers. They may also sell shirts or cups, if they are finished goods made in the United States they are a COGS. Imported beer and wine is <u>not</u> a finished good produced in the United States, unless it's actually bottled in the United States.

Banks

Banks, credit unions, and credit card companies provide services to their clients. They primarily loan money for anything from homes to cars. They also advance funds for credit card transactions and sometimes they even pay you to hold on to your money, although sometimes they charge you. The major COGS they have is labor for tellers at branches, loan processors, customer service via telephone and online chat, and money movers (to fill those ATMs and branches). They have a very minor COGS for credit cards and a declining cost for mailing. To whatever extent the customer service and loan processing is not performed in the United States, it is not a COGS.

Retailers

Many retailers sell products produced by others and run the gambit from grocery stores, clothing stores, car dealerships, gas stations, and hardware stores, to name a few. For most products it is clear where they are produced, although not in every case. Is the food grown in the U.S. or imported? Is the dress made in the U.S. or imported? Was the car assembled in the U.S, if not what is the U.S. content? Was the gasoline refined in the U.S. Where was the lumber cut?

Other retailers sell services such as rental companies of all kinds, insurance companies of all kinds, accounting firms, law firms, transportation companies, construction companies, and entertainment companies. The major COGS for these companies is labor. Transportation companies will have an energy COGS, construction companies will have building materials, and movie theaters will have movie royalties, labor, and food costs.

Manufacturers

Whether the product is for transportation like automobiles, airplanes, trains, boats, rockets, motorcycles, bicycles, wheelchairs, snow mobiles, skateboards, or jet skis; or a household item like refrigerators, sofas, beds, televisions, toasters, tables, toilet paper, or dish soap; or entertainment gadgets like guitars, fishing poles, video games, footballs, tennis rackets, or dolls; or intellectual property like newspapers, magazines, works of art, television programs, movies, or books; it must be created using labor and raw materials.

Manufactured items can be almost completely labor or almost completely raw materials. ***The Best Tax Solution*** determines the COGS based upon where it is finished, the cost of the raw materials and components, and the U.S. content.

Energy Companies

Oil companies, gas and electric utilities, solar power companies, coal mines, wind farms, and hydro-electric dams require large capital investments to produce energy. These investments are necessary infrastructure in order to develop and deliver energy and create income. ***The Best Tax Solution*** does not consider infrastructure a COGS.

An oil company may extract oil from the earth, refine the oil into fuel, and sell the fuel to an airline or gas station. If the oil, natural gas, coal is extracted from the earth in the United States it is a COGS at the earth's surface. Whatever labor, energy, and chemicals needed to bring the commodity to the wellhead is a component of the COGS. Imported oil is not a COGS unless it is refined and then exported as a finished good.

Cost of Sales (COS)

The Best Tax Solution does not consider any marketing costs as a COS. Marketing includes advertising, surveys, and swag, such as pens, cups, t-shirts, tote bags, etc. Retailers have a legitimate COS for sales clerks. COS can be either salaried and/or on a commission basis., For some companies there may be a component for phone or travel. Unreimbursed shipping costs are an integral component of COS for items made in the United States. Imported shipping costs are not a component of COS. Tariffs imposed by foreign countries are a COS and are considered taxes paid to foreign governments.

Dividends

The Best Tax Solution considers dividends paid to stockholders as a cost of doing business. IRS currently taxes the company for profit that is used as a dividend and then taxes the recipient of the dividend. Profit sharing with employees is not a dividend and is not an expense unless it is given to employees that also qualify for COGS or COS. *The Best Tax Solution* does not allow double taxation under any scenario.

Non Profit Entities

A vast majority of non profit entities operate strictly from donations or gifts. However, some organizations have income and currently pay no taxes on their income. These are special interests that cause other taxpayers to pay higher rates. These organizations include anyone who charges dues for membership or receives funds for royalties for use of their name. All monies received by any organization for dues or royalties is income. This would include bar associations, homeowner associations, and special interest organizations, such as AARP and AAA. No exceptions.

Organizations that have investment income are treated as any other individual or company that receives interest, dividends, or other income from market transactions.

Charitable and Religious Entities

Only a small fraction of revenue to charities, churches, synagogs, and mosques is income. For the sake of fairness to other taxpayers and avoid making an exception, only investment income is taxable by *The Best Tax Solution*. Revenue from gifts and donations is not taxable as well as any revenue derived from those gifts or donations. What makes an organization charitable is not only their charter and bylaws, but how they interact with the public. They should be careful when they appear to be competing with for profit companies, high overhead and large salaries are key indicators. Charities that are run for the benefit of employees is anathema to most people.

Trust Funds

Tens of billions of dollars are sheltered from income tax, social security, and medicare by "benevolent" trust funds, causing other taxpayers to make up the difference. Contributions to trust funds are negotiated payments by employers either with a single employer or through a multi-employer plan. These trust funds provide a current or future benefit to an individual or benefit to a class of people in the future. Regardless of how the funds are spent, *The Best Tax Solution* considers contributions to the trust fund as income to the person that is the object of the contribution. Additionally, trust funds receive income from investments such as dividends, interest, and capital gains, just as any individual or company.

Trust funds sustained with gifts or donations are only liable for taxes on their investment income.

Non Governmental Organizations

Any organization, whether for profit or not, that require dues on an hourly, daily, weekly, yearly or any periodic basis are receiving income and subject to *The Best Tax Solution*. These include health clubs, bar associations, homeowner associations, shopping clubs, automobile clubs, retiree organizations, advocacy groups, political parties, and any other entity that charges a periodic fee for membership.

Governmental Organizations

State, county, regional, municipal governments, and quasi-governmental organizations are notorious for avoiding federal taxation. If they compete with the private sector, *The Best Tax Solution* dictates they pay taxes as if they are the private sector. These entities include states, counties, cities, public utilities, golf courses, stadiums, mass transit, parks, and mail delivery, essentially any public service where a fee or tax is charged. Taxes would include property tax, sales tax, license fees, fines, and non-federal income tax. Gone are the days where municipal and state bond measures are deductible to the detriment of the poor and middle class.

Chapter 3 - Winners and Losers

This chapter is by far the most cynical, sarcastic, subjective, and profound in this Volume. Apathy by the electorate, corruption by the ruling political class, narcissism by power hungry politicians, greed by individuals, a self-serving education system, and an unscrupulous malleable media have left this country with 20 trillion dollars of debt and over 100 trillion in unfunded liabilities. In spite of theses shortcomings, the United States is still the greatest country in the annals of history. All the shortcomings can be mitigated by the people as long as there is freedom and the Constitution is observed. Enough of the optimism, on with the rhetoric.

Winners and losers. Shut-up. Fair share. Shut-up. Shared sacrifice. Shut-up Class warfare. Shut-up. Job creators. Shut-up. Throw grandma off the cliff. Shut-up. Global warming/climate change. Shut-up. Right-wingers (conservatives). Shut-up. Left-wingers (liberals). Shut-up Spending problem. Shut-up. Revenue problem. Shut-up. Is there no end to the rhetoric that malevolent politicians will use to get reelected? Probably not. Many Americans are wising up to the rhetoric and whining from both political parties, yet the emotional pulling of heart strings sways enough votes to turn elections. Yet nowhere in the United States Constitution is being emotional and/or ignorant (stupid) discouraged. Politicians use emotion and ignorance to their best advantage to determine winners and losers. In the end most Americans are losers. How should Americans be treated?

The United States has a small document (Constitution) that dictates how people should be treated. Specifically the 14th Amendment states in Section 1:

"All persons born or naturalized in the United States and subject to the jurisdiction thereof, are citizens of the United States and of the State wherein they reside. No State shall make or enforce any law which shall abridge the privileges or immunities of citizens of the United States; nor shall any State deprive any person of life, liberty, or property, without due process of law; nor deny to any person within its jurisdiction the __equal protection__ of the laws."

Equal protection was partially taken away from Americans with the passing of the 16th Amendment. Politicians, lobbyists, and special interests have mostly finished the job with the help of the Supreme Court. For simplicity they will collectively be called social engineers.

A social engineer's primary goal is to affect change either to benefit themselves or their associates (crony capitalists), or in the case of the altruistic social engineer to benefit some segment of society that they "feel" is underrepresented or oppressed (progressives), or in the case of the traditional social engineer to impose their perceived intent of the founding fathers (conservatives). Regardless of their motivations they believe they have the right to pick winners and losers, the Constitution be damned. Social engineers have become increasingly blatant in their pursuit of change. While the crony capitalists, the progressives, and the conservatives are all misguided in one way or another, the truly evil are the crony capitalists. Almost as bad is a combination of a progressive or a conservative and a crony capitalist. Most politicians are not pure crony capitalists, but a mesh with either a progressive or a conservative ideology.

Social engineers use propaganda, apathy, lies, and subterfuge to put policies in place that are antithetical to the fabric of the American society. The tax code is their primary vehicle of choice to maintain power and control over the masses. Fear of the all powerful IRS keeps those not "connected" in their place.

Somewhere along the line, the Supreme Court felt compelled to rule that companies have some Constitutional Rights like people. Where they found that in the Constitution shall remain a mystery for the foreseeable future. The Supreme Court exercises its social engineering by attributing rights to the federal government that were reserved for the states in the Constitution.

Who Determines Winners & Losers

Several elite cliques of social engineers have banded together to formulate a tax code that strokes their ego, promotes social justice, enriches them, controls others, and ensures conformity. Although these cliques may have disparate motivations, the result of their constant micromanagement has spawned a "super-agency", IRS, that is reviled by millions causing fear, anxiety, and grief. Members of this elite political class include crony capitalists, progressives, conservatives, economists, and lobbyists. Their combined efforts accentuate class warfare and are drastically curtailed by *The Best Tax Solution.*

Crony Capitalists

Capitalism is part of the foundation of the United States. Capitalism is not a perfect system but it is the best one ever devised. Capitalism would be almost perfect if every person was righteous, but alas many people are greedy, some are greedy for money and some are greedy for power. Greed cannot be eliminated, but the tax code can and should be constructed to minimize greed, which fuels the crony capitalist. *The Best Tax Solution* helps eliminate cronyism by stopping all tax credits, including those to political contributors and friends of politicians and bureaucrats.

The first step in eradicating crony capitalists is to cut off the spigot of tax credits and tax breaks they get from politicians (Volume II will close the spending for grants and guaranteed loans). How much money do you think crony capitalists would contribute to politicians if they knew there was no tax benefit[3] coming their way? That would also give politicians more time to do the things that the country really needs. Maybe some politicians will actually quit when they lose a perceived power.

Progressives

Generally, progressives honestly believe they are doing as the Constitution says "to form a more perfect Union". The progressive thinks that the Constitution is a living document, that must adapt to the times.

3　Tax benefits are addressed in this Volume of The New Paradigm while Volume II will address other forms of corporate welfare.

They "feel" this way substantially from ignorance of history, the real meaning of the Constitution, and guilt from being successful .Everybody wants progress, who would be against it? Progressives are smarter than other people in that they think they know what is best for other people. Not only do they know what is best for people they also think they know best how to achieve it. When things do not go as they planned, it is because they did not spend enough money on the solution. Can you name the last thing the government did that actually worked? Billions of dollars have been given in tax credits to fight the war on poverty, yet poverty is little better than it was 50 years ago. Can a progressive politician run for office without promising free stuff and lower tax for the middle class and then taxing the wealthy more to pay for it?

Conservatives

Generally, conservatives believe in the original intent of the Constitution and anybody that doesn't is wrong and an ideologue. Whereas progressives think they know what is best for people, conservatives know they know what's best for people. Knowing what's best for people is perhaps more dangerous than thinking so. Personal responsibility is the earmark of the conservative, even if you grew up in an environment where you never learned personal responsibility. Conservatives can not seem to picture societal interactions outside their personal frame of reference. Can a conservative politician run without promising to cut taxes for some special interest group, such as small businesses or the middle class?

Economists

Academia, government agencies and committees, and private non-profit organizations are chock-full of economists with doctorates and little, if any, first hand experience with running a business or creating jobs. They influence government policy with their superior intellect and sophisticated JAMS (Just Another Modeling System). Virtually all economists have preconceived opinions on economic policy and theories driven by either their ideology or ego, even more so for academia. A few of the government entities establishing or influencing policy include the Federal Reserve, Office of Management and Budget (OMB), Congressional Budget Office (CBO), U.S. Treasury Department, Joint Committee on Taxation (JCT), Social Security Administration (SSA),

Bureau of Economic Analysis, Census Bureau, Council of Economic Advisers, Bureau of Labor Statistics, Commerce Department, and the Labor Department. Talk about redundancy and a plethora of TLAs (Three Letter Acronyms).

The non-profit Tax Foundation is the oldest tax policy think tank in the United States. Many of the charts and graphs included in this book are courtesy of the Tax Foundation. Since 1937, their stated purpose is to "educate taxpayers about sound tax policy and the size of the tax burden borne by Americans at all levels of government." The foundation has a robust modeling system named Taxes and Growth (TAG) Model that is used by citizens, journalists, and Members of Congress to help assess the impact of changes to tax policy. While this may be one of the best models for evolutionary tax proposals, it is totally inadequate for a revolutionary tax proposal like ***The Best Tax Solution***. For those interested in furthering their education on taxes, a visit to their website at taxfoundation.org is well worth the effort.

Tax Analysts at tax.org is also a valuable information source for understanding what is happening pertaining to taxes worldwide and the history of taxes in the United States. They not only provide information but also employ legal resources to keep the government transparent.

Not all economists are wrong, but an example of their thinking can be found in Alan Coles's conclusion in his article for the Tax Foundation of August 1, 2016 titled *Corporate and Individual Tax Expenditures 2016* which reads:

"It is therefore important to remember that a haphazard elimination of every tax expenditure, regardless of kind, would be misguided. Not all tax expenditures are equally worthy of elimination. It is important to ask, for each expenditure, whether it serves a reasonable purpose and whether it accomplishes that purpose in a reasonable way. This trillion-dollar area of the tax code deserves examination and a degree of healthy skepticism, but it doesn't deserve across-the-board elimination."

Why would elimination of every tax expenditure be misguided?

Why are some worthy of elimination and others are not? Why is it important to ask whether a tax expenditure serves a reasonable purpose? Is Mr. Cole the person deciding if a purpose is reasonable or is it a government bureaucrat? Likewise, does Mr. Cole or the government bureaucrat decide if it is accomplishing the purpose in a reasonable way? Agreed, this trillion dollar area of the tax code deserves examination and a degree of healthy skepticism, but why doesn't it deserve across-the-board elimination? Would economists still respect Mr. Cole's conclusion if he did not "feel" that way? Nothing personal Mr. Cole, just anecdotal.

Lobbyists

Framers of the United States Constitution contemplated lobbyists before they penned the document. James Madison wrote in Federalist[4] 10 about factions stating: "The latent causes of faction are thus sown in the nature of man". Madison postulated on majority factions and minority factions. Majority factions are political parties, Democratic Party and Republican Party, hence partisan politics. Minority factions are special interest groups, hence lobbyists. Madison reasoned that the only way to limit the damage that may be caused by a faction is to limit it's effect on the Republic.

James Madison

What the Framers did not foresee was the evolution of the lobbyist from a faction of people to the special interest lobbyist of a group of corporations or a single company. After all, people vote not companies. They also never envisaged a time when a single lobbyist could afford to influence (bribe) many delegates. Lobbyists might serve a purpose, but should have no sway over the tax code. Taxing power is reserved for defense of the country and the "general welfare". Nowhere in Article I of the Constitution is Congress permitted to levy taxes allowing special welfare. James Madison would roll over in his grave if he saw the damage caused by the modern day lobbyist and the lack of character by Congressmen and Senators.

---

4   The Federalist Papers initiated by Alexander Hamilton with James Madison writing Federalist 10. The Federalist Papers should be read by anyone who wants a full understanding of the Constitution.

More than 12,000 registered lobbyists and approximately 100,000 people are involved in lobbying Congress primarily for preferential tax treatment. An authoritative analysis of the lobbying industry was undertaken by James A. Thurber, a distinguished professor and Director of the Center for Congressional and Presidential Studies at American University, where he was the principal investigator of a four-year study of lobbying and ethics for the Committee for Economic Development and is working with

James A. Thurber

The Organization for Economic Co-operation and Development (OECD-Paris) on international lobbying and ethics reform.

Class Warfare

Pandering to the middle class is what politicians do best, because that is where the votes are. Tax credits and deductions are promised by politicians to families with children, working people, and small businesses. What about couples without children and single people? Who are the mysterious working people? And what small businesses are worthy of tax breaks? Does anyone really believe that a politician is motivated by their compassion for the voter they are courting? Taxpayers must learn that there is no proverbial free lunch. When a tax break is doled out, it is invariably accompanied by an increase on some other taxpayer. This constant manipulation of the tax code creates friction and division between the poor, middle class, and rich alike. The net effect is to generate more income inequality and animosity because the more money a taxpayer has, the more lawyers, accountants, and politicians they can afford.

Taxpayers are highly vested in their tax breaks. Middle class with their home mortgage deduction, child tax credits, retirement accounts, health savings accounts, and education savings accounts, to name a few. Poor working people with their earned income credits. Small businesses with their depreciation and expense write-offs. Hedge fund managers with their preferential tax treatment. And large multinational companies with everything under the sink. Any guess who the winners are with this eclectic assortment of taxpayers? If it weren't for the pandering by politicians of the middle class for their votes, the taxpayers with the best lobbyists would be the only winners. Occasionally politicians will throw the poor and middle class a bone, otherwise the benefits in the tax code go to the big dogs with the most effective lobbyists.

Tax Expenditures

Assistant Secretary of the Treasury Stanley S. Surrey came up with a method of determining the spending effect on the budget detailed in the tax code with tax breaks, loopholes, tax credits, deductions, and other preferences. Although Secretary Surrey proposed this procedure in 1967 it was not codified until The Congressional Budget and Impoundment Control Act of 1974. Through this act came the Congressional Budget Office and the definition of tax expenditures as "those revenue losses attributable to provisions of the Federal tax laws which allow a special exclusion, exemption, or deduction from gross income or which provide a special credit, a preferential rate of tax, or a deferral of tax liability". Tax expenditures of $1.2 trillion annually are roughly equal to the combined budgets of Medicare (not including Medicaid) and the military budget, $595 billion and $604 billion

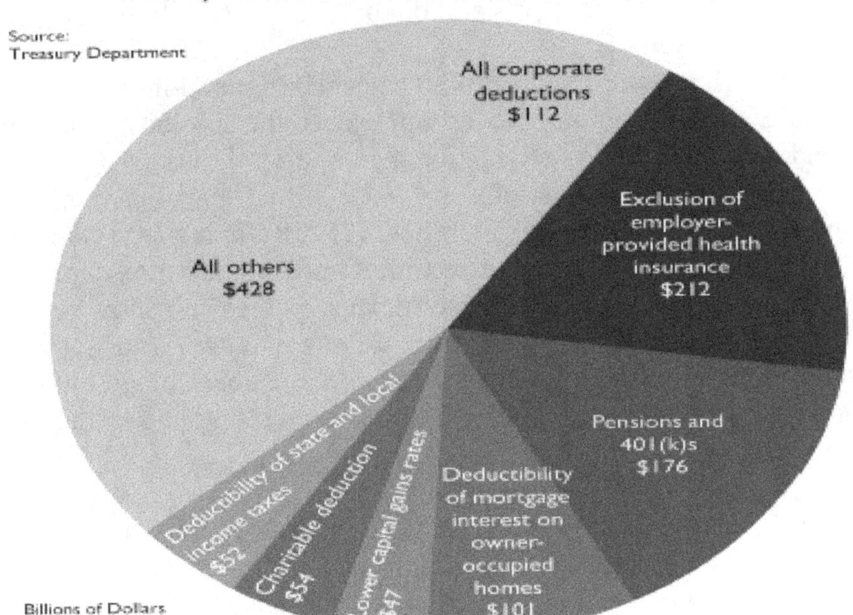

respectively. Social engineers just can not get away from spending. With *The Best Tax Solution* all tax expenditures will cease and the incorrigible Congress will have to spend taxpayer money the old fashion way, by appropriating for specific purposes. What will the politicians do when their spending is brought out in the light? The only reason tax rates are so high is to support tax expenditures that spend more than 1/3 of the revenue raised by the IRS.

Tax Credits

Surprise. Surprise. The New Deal of the 1930s ushered in the concept of tax credits. Politicians and crony capitalists, with prodding from special interests, determine how America and its people will conform to norms they deem utopic. Giving tax credits is inherently unconstitutional. The difference between a tax credit and a deduction is that a tax credit directly reduces the tax liability and deductions reduce the taxable income. Collectively they are called tax breaks and/or loopholes and are insidious to a fair society. The taxing power given Congress in Article I of the Constitution insists that all indirect taxes must be uniform. Even the 16th Amendment doesn't change the uniformity of taxes, it only allows for progressive rates. But, politicians must be able to do "good" for their constituents and donors, the Constitution be damned.

Modern tax credits can be categorized as nonrefundable and refundable. Refundable tax credits can exceed the amount of tax actually paid and have been called a negative income tax. Politicians instituted a temporary negative income tax in 1975 with <u>bipartisan</u> support and expanded it and made it permanent in 1978. Refundable tax credits are primarily for low and moderate income families and were implemented by social engineers, a.k.a. gutless politicians, so they can show how much welfare has been reduced. If it looks like welfare, and spends like welfare, then it's welfare. One of the main goals of *The Best Tax Solution* is to stop politicians from social engineering and spending with the tax code.

While most individuals taxpayers are thrilled with their tax credit of the earned income tax credit (EITC), the child tax credit (CTC), and energy efficient tax credits, they are still the losers. The real winners are the businesses whose tax credits include the following:

- General business credit of which there are 36
- Carryback and carryforward of unused credits
- Alcohol, etc., used as fuel

- Bio-diesel and renewable diesel used as fuel
- Credit for increasing research activities
- Employee stock ownership credit
- Low-income housing credit
- Enhanced oil recovery credit
- Expenditures to provide access to disabled individuals
- Electricity produced from certain renewable resources, etc
- Indian employment credit
- Credit for portion of employer social security taxes paid with respect to employee cash tips

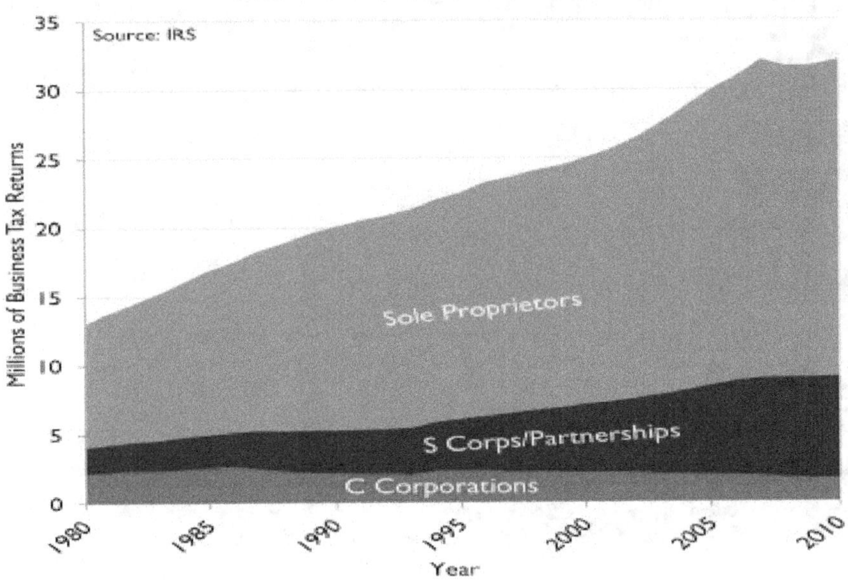

- Clinical testing expenses for certain drugs for rare diseases or conditions
- New markets tax credit
- Small employer pension plan start-up costs
- Employer-provided child care credit
- Railroad track maintenance credit
- Credit for production of low sulfur diesel fuel
- Credit for producing oil and gas from marginal wells

- Credit for producing fuel from a non conventional source
- Credit for production from advanced nuclear power facilities
- New energy efficient home credit
- Energy efficient appliance credit
- Mine rescue team training credit
- Agricultural chemicals security credit
- Employer wage credit for employees who are active duty members of the uniformed services
- Credit for carbon dioxide sequestration
- Employee health insurance expenses of small employers.

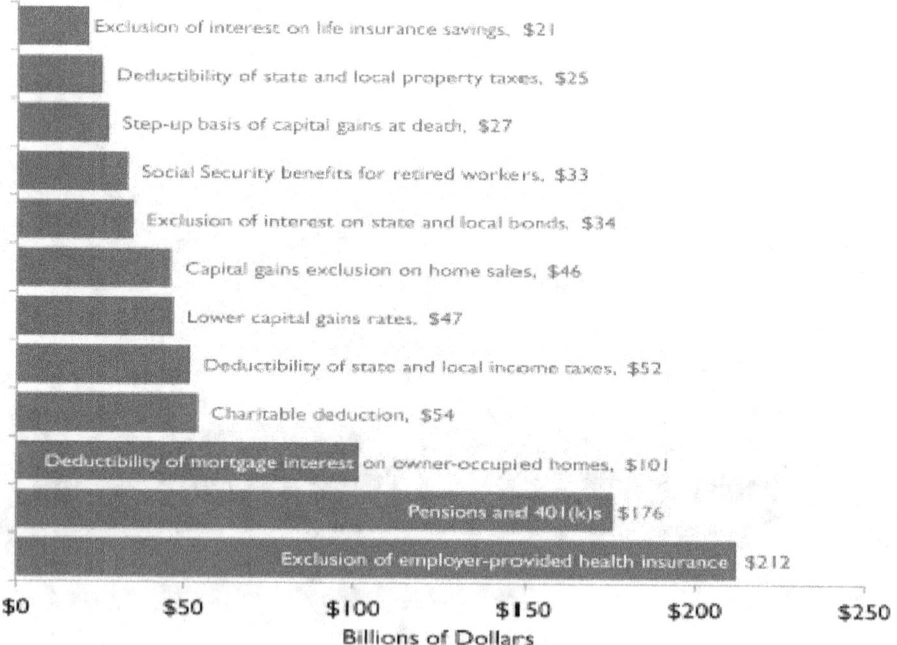

As if that was not enough, businesses add the sum of these credits, regardless of the size of the company or sum of the credits. It's no wonder some companies pay no taxes. With *The Best Tax Solution* all tax credits for individuals and companies would cease to exist. Individuals should have no qualms of foregoing their miniscule tax credits to create a fair playing field and put a few lobbyists out of business.

Tax credits cover the gambit from retirement contributions, alternative fuel, electric vehicle, healthcare, making work pay, plug-in vehicle, solar energy, education, children, and earned income. Does anybody really think that politicians can decide what is best for people?

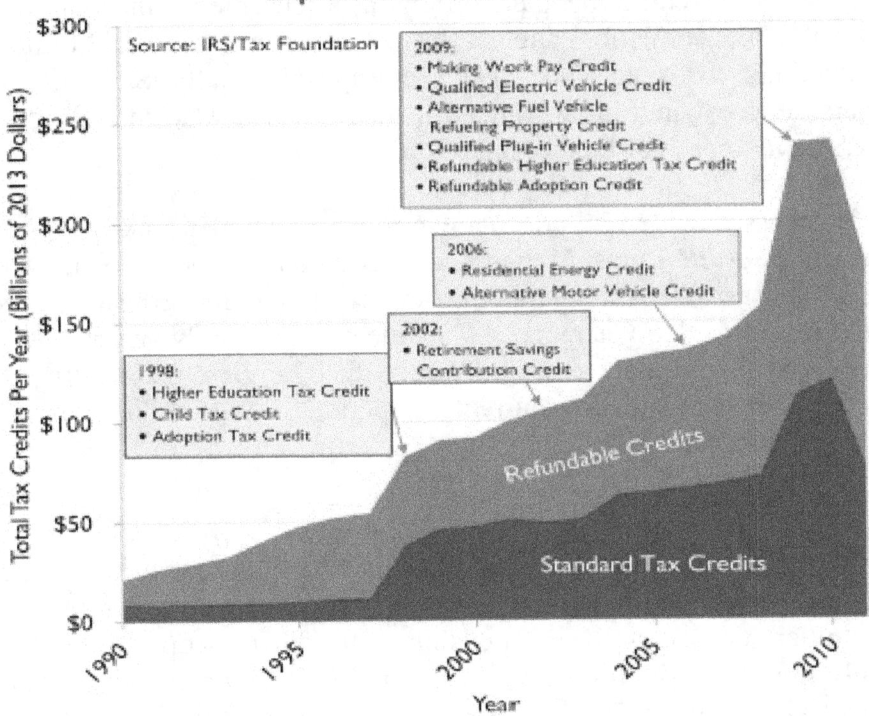

Refundable tax credits have surged since their introduction in the 1970s. Higher education tax credits, child tax credits, and adoption tax credits were boosted with the Taxpayer Relief Act of 1997. Since 1990, refundable tax credits have soared from less than $20 billion to nearly $150 billion currently. Overall, tax credits of all kinds are one of the largest domestic spending programs. Neither major political party is immune to insidious spending by doling out tax credits.

Deductions

Like tax credits, deductions have their winners and their losers. While tax credits, directly lower the tax liability, deductions lower the taxable income of a taxpayer. Homeowners believe they are set because they can deduct the interest on their home mortgage to the tune of $101 billion annually. Is that fair to the renter or the poor person who has to pay a large portion of their paycheck for payroll taxes? Does anybody with a house care if it is fair? Contributions to charities amount to $54 billion for those that itemize deductions. Why should taxpayers who do not make enough to itemize have to subsidize feelings of guilt by wealthy taxpayers? Will wealthy people stop giving to charities if they can not write it off? Deductions for state and local income taxes cost $52 billion and deductions for state and local property taxes tally $25 billion. Taxpayers choose where they want to live and work, why should other taxpayers have to pay for their choices?

Businesses can and do deduct every expense under the sun. With *The Best Tax Solution* most of their deductions go away because they are getting a lower tax rate and the money they may waste in overhead affects their bottom line. See Chapter 2 – Income to see how businesses will determine what legitimate expenses are with *The Best Tax Solution*. Their deductions and credits currently amount to $115 billion in tax expenditures annually.

Exemptions

A couple with 8 children gets many more exemptions then a single person with one child. Nobody told the couple to have 8 children. Should other taxpayers be responsible for other peoples children especially since 60% of all taxpayers are single? Clergymen and veterans enjoy special exemptions. Is not career choice a personal decision? If a veteran needs an exemption, why can't they get it from the veterans administration or a special welfare program? Charitable and religious organizations are exempt from taxes even if they directly compete with for profit companies. Throw in the exempt state and local entities that are exempt and real money is involved.

Exceptions

Payments for municipal and state bonds amount to another $34 billion annually. These exceptions may be classified as an exclusion, but at least they are not also deductible by an employer, subtle and totally inconsequential difference. Interest on life insurance savings adds another $21 billion. Social Security benefits for retired workers create another exception of $33 billion. Capital gains exception on home sales comes to $46 billion. Adding the $27 billion lost with the step-up basis of capital gains at death and substantial revenues are never realized. *Ka-ching, ka-ching.*

Exclusions

Employer provided health insurance is excluded from income and accounts for the largest single tax expenditure of $215 billion annually. Close behind is the $176 billion exclusion for pension and 401K contributions. Not only are exclusions not taxable, but they are deductible for the employer, a double whammy.

Preferences

Whether a tax break or loophole is a tax credit, deduction, exemption, exclusion, or a preference is mainly semantics. One taxpayer's exemption is another taxpayer's exclusion. Preferences are an anathema to fairness, whether it is the lower tax rate for capital gains costing $47 billion or the 200 preferences cloaked in the disguise of tax credits, deductions, exemptions, exceptions, or exclusions. *The Best Tax Solution* eliminates them all in one fell swoop.

Regressive Taxes

Impacting low income and middle income taxpayers more than wealthy taxpayers and corporations regressive taxes are eliminated by The Best Tax Solution. In the last 75 years the federal government revenues have moved from 65% regressive to about 40%. Income tax in

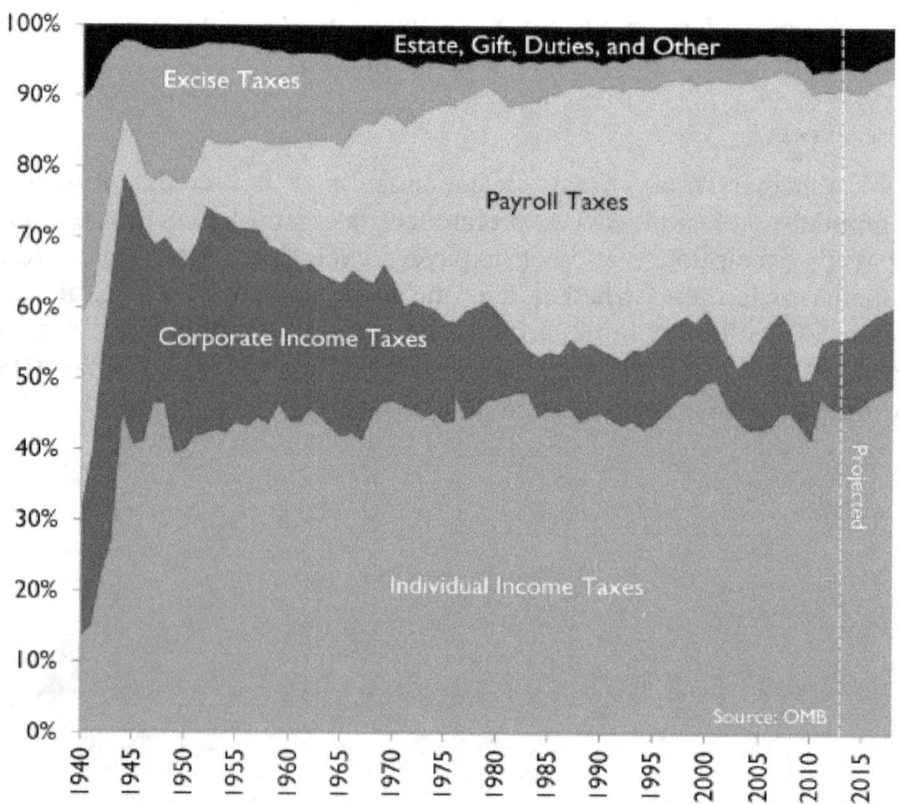

the current tax code is progressive, but payroll taxes remain a regressive tax. With The Best Tax Solution payroll taxes are removed from the regressive tax column into the proportional tax category. That leaves the remaining regressive taxes a small percentage of total government revenue. Eliminating excise taxes, government fees, duties, estate taxes, and gift taxes will simplify tax collection and make more wealthy taxpayers pay their fair share, not to mention the animosity and anger from   low and fixed income taxpayers when rates are inevitably increased.

States should be the domain of regressive taxes like sales tax, gasoline tax, property tax, and estate taxes.

Excise Taxes

IRS completely disregards Article I Section 8 of the Constitution which states: *"all Duties, Imposts and Excises shall be uniform throughout the United States"*. Publication 510 from the IRS is replete with 60 pages of exclusions, exceptions, refunds, and credits, spitting in the face of the Constitution. The burden of paying, cost of compliance, and unconstitutional application of excise taxes are reason enough to eliminate them. Who wouldn't want an 18 cent reduction in the gasoline tax? Who wouldn't want excise taxes on telephone usage removed? Who wouldn't want to stop airfare taxes? What fisherman wants to keep the excise tax on sport fishing equipment, fishing rods, electric outboard motors, and fishing tackle boxes? Would archers be willing to not be taxed on bows, quivers, and arrow shafts. How about tires, gas guzzlers, and vaccines? What about coal, do you think it may affect your electricity bill? Do truckers really want to pay the 12% retail tax on their chassis, bodies, and trailers? With *The Best Tax Solution* all federal excise taxes are repealed.

Government Fees

IRS is somewhat illiterate. They don't seem to understand English. Theoretically, excise taxes are "inland taxes" being they apply to products and commodities sold in the United States, whereas duties and imposts are applied at the border. Why then does the ship passenger pay an excise fee to get on the cruise ship? No place in the Constitution under Congressional taxing power does it allow fees. Fees such as TSA security fees at the airport, passport fees at the Post Office, entrance fee for National Parks, fees for copyrights and patents, and fees from IRS and virtually every government agency to "defray expenses". Shouldn't any American be entitled to equal services from the federal government? Can you imagine the savings realized by not paying and collecting fees? With *The Best Tax Solution* all federal service fees are repealed.

Duties

Imposts or duties are defined by U.S. Customs and Border Protection as "a tariff or tax imposed on goods when transported across international borders. The purpose of Customs Duty is to protect each country's economy, residents, jobs, environment, etc., by controlling the flow of goods, especially restrictive and prohibited goods, into and out of the country." Duties are defined by *The Best Tax Solution* as money paid to the United States for importing goods by American citizens and corporations. Further, tariffs are defined as money paid foreign governments for exporting or importing goods. The United States has no authority to dictate to foreign governments tariffs they charge for goods not covered by trade agreements. In lieu of free trade, reciprocal tariffs are highly recommended by *The Best Tax Solution.* With *The Best Tax Solution* all duties are repealed.

Estate Taxes

Many economists may not consider estate taxes as a regressive tax in that it does not affect low income taxpayers. But what it does is destroy family businesses and favor the very wealthy who have unlimited lawyers and accountants to help avoid estate taxes. What is the difference between a federal tax on an asset such as property and an asset that remains after death? Eventually all assets are sold and income is derived from the sale. Additionally, there is no chance of double taxation. With *The Best Tax Solution* all federal estate taxes are repealed and the step-up of asset basis is scrapped.

Gift Taxes

Double taxation with *The Best Tax Solution* is a nonstarter. Charities, waitresses and waiters, taxi drivers, and other people who live on tips are not so wealthy as to have a significant impact on the federal revenues. Also, these gifts are no longer deductible with *The Best Tax Solution*. For a further discussion on gift taxes see Chapter 2 – Income.

Chapter 4 - Consequences of The Best Tax Solution

The tax code, like any other law, has consequences on behavior, whether intended or unintended. The current tax code is designed to convey favor upon special-interest groups and bribe voters to help reelect existing politicians. There is little thought given to consequences outside of the next election. It may appear cynical, but a thorough analysis of the current tax code reveals few altruistic provisions. Provisions are for special interests or classes of potential voters. When a provision is not implemented to influence behavior, it is implemented to reward campaign contributors or buy votes. In either case it is social engineering run amok.

To the extent that a tax provision is implemented to influence or nudge a person's actions it is a flagrant infringement upon liberty. Nowhere in the Constitution or the Declaration of Independence is the government endowed with the authority to dictate individual pursuits. With *The Best Tax Solution* the entire concept follows a proprietary modeling methodology known as **SHOPPING**. All aspects of *The Best Tax Solution* follow the **SHOPPING** model.

SHOPPING is an acronym for a series of steps that help ensure success. First step is establishing a **P**urpose, which is a general direction or vector. Second step is creating **G**oals and objectives, which corresponds to this chapter of intended consequences. Third step is setting **P**olicies and procedures, which reflect values enshrined in the Constitution. Fourth step is formulating a **S**trategy to achieve the goals of *The Best Tax Solution,* as detailed in Chapter 6 – Implementing. Fifth step is **H**uman resources, that accounts for people affected such as taxpayers and personnel required to implement and run the Income System. Sixth step is **N**umeration, to measure success and adjust parameters. The first six steps can take place and still not ensure success without step seven of **I**nnovation, which is the essence of *The New Paradigm* described in Chapter 1. Step eight leaves nothing else to do but to put it in **O**peration, and realize the benefits to America. **SHOPPING** is an easy to understand and remember methodology that can be used for government, personal, and business success. Again, but not in order, **SHOPPING** is:

- *S* trategy
- *H* uman Resources
- *O* perations
- *P* urpose
- *P* olicies and Procedures
- *I* nnovation
- *N* umeration
- *G* oals and Objectives

The **Purpose** of ***The Best Tax Solution*** is succinctly stated in Chapter 1 as creating: **<u>A fair and simple income tax for taxpayers.</u>**

Goals and Objectives

Goals and objectives are quantitative/economic and/or qualitative/personal liberty. Quantitatively *The Best Tax Solution* is designed to provide all of the following:

- average economic growth of 4% or more per year for 10 years,
- $2.5 trillion in capital repatriation in first 3 years,
- average job growth of more than 3,000,000 per year for 5 years,
- balanced budget within 3 years,
- 75% reduction in tax compliance overhead within 2 years,
- 10% increase in new business formation per year for 5 years,
- national debt reduction by 5% per year after 3 years,
- elimination of $1.2 trillion in annual tax expenditures,
- elimination of $20 billion in fraudulent refunds,
- 20% increase in dividend distributions per year,
- average 10% increase in manufacturing per year for 5 years.

Qualitatively *The Best Tax Solution* is designed to provide all of the following:

- extension of Social Security solvency by at least 50 years,
- extension of Medicare solvency by at least 50 years,
- elimination of 75,000 pages from the Internal Revenue Code within 2 years,
- reassignment or layoff of 98,000 IRS employees within 3 years,
- 20% reduction in tax attorneys and tax accountants within 3 years,
- 5% reduction of people in poverty per year,
- 100% elimination of federal excise taxes, including gasoline, within 3 years,
- 100% elimination of federal government fees within 2 years,
- 50% elimination of duties within 2 years, 100% within 5 years,
- 25% increase of energy production within 5 years,
- repeal of the 16th Amendment within 7 years.

Quantitative/Economic Goals

Key to reducing the national debt of 20 trillion dollars is by having economic growth of at least 4% on an annual basis for the foreseeable future. Essential for economic growth is creating an environment of business certainty which will promote new business formation. In order to facilitate business formation, capital is required and there is no faster way than capital repatriation. Trillions of dollars are overseas and with *The Best Tax Solution* much of it will be brought back to the United States. Bringing back capital and reverse inversion will provide more than enough incentive to produce millions of jobs with higher wages.

Budget deficits strip capital from the private sector and continue to raise the national debt. Also stripping the private sector of wealth is an estimated $140 billion spent each year by taxpayers complying with the onerous tax code. Tax compliance is a hindrance to new business formation and a drain on productivity and competitiveness. Deficits are compounded by over a trillion dollars in tax expenditures and billions in fraudulent refunds and payments.

Economic Growth

Maintaining economic growth of at least 4% a year for the foreseeable future is essential to eliminating the budget deficit, reducing the national debt, and bolstering Social Security and Medicare. For the last 8 years economic growth has averaged less than 2% a year because of shortsighted tax policy, over regulation, and misguided social experiments. *The Best Tax Solution* will fix the tax policy and some of the over regulation and social experiments. Volume II of the *New Paradigm* will address the misguided social experiments and Volume III will tackle the over regulation.

Lower tax rates and more certainty by businesses assure an environment conducive to economic growth and business formation. Removing some of the burden of tax compliance on society will allow billions of hours currently spent attempting to comply with an archaic tax system to be used for leisure or to grow the economy.

Capital Repatriation

Repatriation of capital will provide an initial spurt in economic growth that will be maintained with lower tax rates and savings of billions of dollars in tax compliance. Economic growth will continue as business costs for labor are reduced by lower payroll taxes, less expense on excise taxes, and increased consumer spending with individuals realizing higher take home pay. Business and individuals will no longer make decisions based on the tax code, because there is nothing they can do to reduce tax liability other than pay more in dividends, pay more in wages, upgrade plants and equipment, and/or manufacture with more United States content. Businesses will become more efficient and profitable knowing there are overhead expenses they can no longer deduct.

Benefits from capital repatriation will provide numerous positive results, including additional tax revenue from dividend distributions, orders for new equipment, new plant construction and upgrades, and massive job creation. Because *The Best Tax Solution* eliminates all depreciation of assets and allows manufacturing plants and equipment cost as COGS, thus reducing taxable income, corporations will be more likely to purchase plants and equipment with cash instead of borrowing. New dividend distributions will increase revenue to entrepreneurs, investors, trust funds, and individuals.

The vast majority of businesses are either sole proprietors, partnerships, or Sub-chapter S corporations and are taxed at individual tax rates. From the IRS website:

"S corporations are corporations that elect to pass corporate income, losses, deductions, and credits through to their shareholders for federal tax purposes. Shareholders of S corporations report the

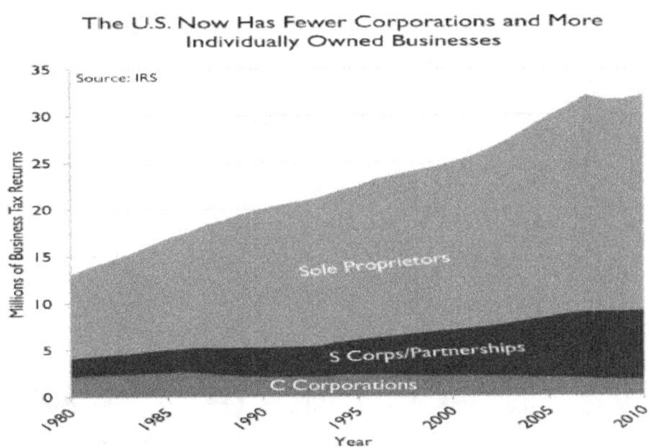

flow-through of income and losses on their personal tax returns and are assessed tax at their individual income tax rates. This allows S corporations to avoid double taxation on the corporate income. S corporations are responsible for tax on certain built-in gains and passive income at the entity level."

S Corporations are closely held domestic corporations with no more than 100 shareholders that are formed to avoid double taxation by making election under Sub-chapter S Chapter 1 Subtitle-A of the Internal Revenue Code (IRC). Definition of a C Corporation in the IRC can only come from a bureaucrat. IRC states '...*the term "C corporation" means, with respect to any taxable year, a corporation which is not an S corporation...*'. You can't make this up. With **The Best Tax Solution**, since tax rates are the same for all entities, the election to be an S Corp versus C Corp is superfluous. Likewise there is no difference between a partnership and a L.L.C. (Limited Liability Corporation). The only decision will be whether to be a Sole Proprietor or a corporation. Because dividends paid by a corporation reduce income and are only taxable to the recipient of the dividend with **The Best Tax Solution**, more capital will flow to stockholders that can be used for savings, consuming, or new business formation. New simplicity and less punitive tax rates will create more business certainty which is essential to business expansion.

Job Growth

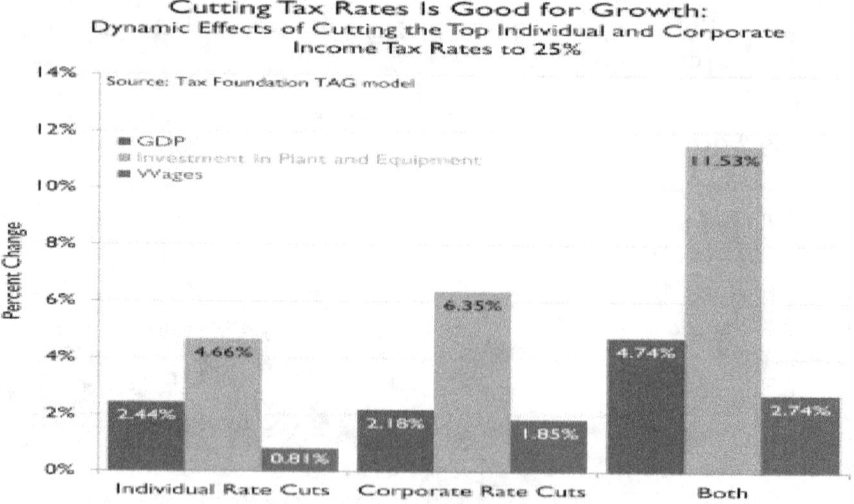

Small business growth generated by business certainty will free entrepreneurs to take a calculated risk, instead of a hope and a prayer. Imagine small businesses not being concerned about 35% tax rates, federal excise taxes, and punitive payroll taxes. They would have lower accounting fees and lower labor costs (through reduced payroll taxes), that they can use to expand, pay higher wages, provide additional benefits, or turn a profit and stay in business. With new business formation comes jobs and economic growth. Jobs that are new taxpayers and higher demand for workers, that generate higher wages.

Corporate inversion will become history when companies discover they can bring back unlimited profits to pay dividends. Companies will also have lower manufacturing costs through the because of lower payroll taxes and the definition of COGS (see Chapter 2 – Income) with American content, lower energy costs, lower accounting and legal fees, and lower tax rate compared to most industrialized countries. Indeed with lower tax rates there will be a reverse inversion, with companies that had previously received better tax treatment abroad, calculating higher return on investment with United States based production. Domestic corporations will still produce products overseas, but that will be mostly for foreign consumption.

Out-sourcing will be greatly stifled because with *The Best Tax Solution* out-sourcing will no longer be a COGS or COS (Cost of Sales), enhancing domestic job growth.

Balanced Budget

By reducing tax expenditures of $1.5 trillion, lowering tax rates, expanding the tax base, and reducing government spending by eliminating tax collection overhead, revenues will increase dramatically. The drain on the budget by Social Security and Medicare will be nipped in the bud. By default *The Best Tax Solution* rescinds the Affordable Care Act, aka Obamacare, saving an additional $30 billion per year in administrative costs. There is nothing the government administers that can not be done better and less costly by the private sector.

Reduced Cost of Tax Compliance

The National Taxpayers Union estimated that taxpayers spend

over \$230 billion and over 6 billion hours complying with the tax code, not even counting the millions of hours by government employees processing the paperwork. This cost directly impacts productivity and economic growth. Even IRS's National Taxpayer Advocate Nina Olson stated: "… I believe we need fundamental tax reform, sooner rather than later, so the entire system does not implode." IRS imposes nearly 75% of the total paperwork burden by all government agencies combined. The tax code is so complex that almost 95% of all taxpayers have to hire a third party to file a somewhat correct tax return. Vast new complexities were added by president Obama's signature legislative "accomplishment". Over 3,300 pages of IRS regulations, treasury decisions, notices, revenue procedures, and revenue rulings were added by the Patient Protection and Affordable Care Act (Obamacare), as if the tax code was not complex enough. Describing IRS as a "super agency" is not an exaggeration it's an understatement. Within two years *The Best Tax Solution* will reduce the taxpayers' cost of compliance by 75%, causing a surge in productivity, business profits, and increased government revenues. After 5 years the cost of compliance will be reduced by 90%.

New Business Formation

Several factors influence creation of new businesses, not the least of which is the prospect of success. In order to facilitate an environment conducive to a successful business, businesses require a degree of certainty, a viable market, an adequate supply of labor, and possibly capital investment. Business certainty can be provided by the government tax policy and limited regulation. *The Best Tax Solution* resolves the tax policy part of the equation. Any entrepreneur worth their salt would be willing to take a risk given a stable tax policy and a knowable set of regulations. Currently more businesses are failing rather than being formed because of the punitive tax policy and over regulation. Taxpayers will have to wait for Volume III of The New Paradigm to fix the over regulation, but new businesses will increase 10% per year with implementation of *The Best Tax Solution*.

National Debt Reduction

In 3 years, after the budget comes into balance, the national debt of \$20 trillion must be aggressively reduced, not to mention the \$120 trillion in unfunded liabilities. The income tax rate of 10%, the initial rate proposed by *The Best Tax Solution*, is artificially inflated in order to quickly bring the budget into balance and thereafter provide one trillion dollars per year for paying off the national debt. Once the national debt is eliminated, the income tax rate can be reduced to a more appropriate 7% - 8%. By periodically adjusting the income tax rate and the subsistence level, all contingencies can be dealt with by *The Best Tax Solution*.

Unfunded liabilities of $120 trillion are a popular misconception in that it assumes that all future Social Security and Medicare benefit due have no corresponding revenue. For that to happen, the government would have to stop collecting Social Security and Medicare taxes, which is not likely to occur. Someday those social programs may be replaced, but by that time the unfunded liabilities will be inconsequential.

Elimination of Tax Expenditures

When Americans realize that what Ronald Reagan said at his first inaugural address is as true today as it was on January 20, 1981. President Reagan said: "In this present crisis, government is not the solution to our problem; government is the problem." Government is constantly social engineering and their favorite tool is through the Internal Revenue Code via tax expenditures. Over 1.2 trillion dollars are dispensed each year by the government through tax credits, deductions, exceptions, exemptions, and compromises. Collectively, they are all loopholes eliminated with *The Best Tax Solution*. If Congress wants to spend money, let them do it the way the Constitution dictates, appropriate the money so that Americans can see real transparency. Another Reagan gem: "Government's view of the economy could be summed up in a few short phrases: If it moves, tax it. If it keeps moving, regulate it. And if it stops moving, subsidize it."

Elimination of Fraudulent Refunds

IRS estimates that in 2016 at least $21 billion will be lost through fraudulent refunds and bogus tax credits, a huge increase from $6.5 billion in 2013. Some of these are innocent mistakes, but the majority is from taxpayers who actually cheat, surprise. Most of the fraudulent refunds are from 2 main sources; taxpayers who claim invalid deductions and identity thieves who file income tax returns with falsified W2s to either receive bogus refunds or Earned Income Tax Credits from people that did not file because they did not believe they owed taxes or were entitled to a refund. The preferred vehicle for thieves is the use of prepaid cards. Sheer incompetence by the IRS and the overly complex tax code are the primary reasons for the fraud. With *The Best Tax Solution* there are no deductions, no W2s, and no tax credits, which together with multi-factor authentication will eliminate these methods for perpetuating fraud.

Increase of Dividends

Because there is no double taxation with *The Best Tax Solution*, companies will be much more inclined to pay dividends to stockholders instead of paying taxes. Currently, dividends are paid on after tax profits, unlike *The Best Tax Solution* which directly reduces taxable income. An influx to shareholders of dividend income will create more capital for savings, new business formation, consumer spending, or reinvestment. The goal is to increase dividend distributions by 20% or more over current levels. Dividends being non taxable to corporations will repatriate billions of dollars annually that would otherwise remain overseas, proverbially killing two birds with one stone.

Increase in Manufacturing

In light of the increased capital repatriation, the ability to immediately expense manufacturing facilities and equipment, and reduced manufacturing costs, manufacturing will increase an average of 10% a year for 10 years, at least until other countries adopt a tax policy similar to *The Best Tax Solution*. Domestic manufacturing costs will decrease when the payroll tax for the employer drops to 5% from 7.65% and the elimination of excise taxes on energy and other raw materials. Also driving the growth in domestic manufacturing will be reduced profits on international manufacturing, vast capital repatriation, and the ability to immediately expense manufacturing facilities and manufacturing equipment. Because international manufacturing of products for import to the United States have a different cost structure based on American content, corporations will be less willing to manufacture overseas and import to the United States, knowing they will pay more in taxes even though labor rates may be lower overseas.

Some qualitative goals are more esoteric and are never fully achievable even with *The Best Tax Solution*. Regardless of how much improvement is made in these esoteric goals, there will always be dissatisfaction with the result because they are very subjective. Subjective goals include political accountability, end of class warfare, income inequality, personal liberty, personal savings, and financial liberty.

Increased political accountability is promoted by limiting what politicians can vote on without transparency. With *The Best Tax Solution* the American taxpayer will know precisely where their elected representative <u>stands</u> and <u>votes</u> on income tax rate, Social Security tax rate, Medicare tax rate, and the minimum subsistence level. Elimination of all deductions, credits, excise taxes, government fees, and the IRS will give politicians no room to hide from the electorate, reduce susceptibility to special interest influence, and give them more time to deal with pressing problems.

War is constantly being waged between the poor, middle class, and rich, usually to the detriment of the poor and middle class. Chapter 5 – Scenarios shows what each class can expect under *The Best Tax Solution* implemented in totality. No class will be treated differently, and is that not the definition of fair? Currently the tax code is "rigged" for those with the best lobbyists, attorneys, and accountants. Will the rich be able to maintain their advantage when they have to play by the same rules as everyone else?

When corporations can no longer deduct multimillion dollar executive salaries and must pay 5% Social Security on all their earnings, will stockholders tolerate the exorbitant costs? Income inequality will be dramatically evened out with vastly lower payroll taxes on the poor and lower middle class. *The Best Tax Solution* will not completely eliminate income inequality, but it will put a dent in the situation and give everyone a fair opportunity by playing by the same rules.

Currently the IRS mandates that every taxpayer keep detailed records for any expenses they may wish to deduct or receive a credit.

News flash! What right does the government have to know how you spend your money? It is not in the Constitution. ***The Best Tax Solution*** by eliminating deductions, tax credits, excise taxes, and government fees gives taxpayers personal liberty to spend as they see fit without social engineering by the government and the burdensome collection of receipts for future audits.

Social engineers, aka politicians, dictate what taxpayers should save, whether it be health savings, education savings, or retirement savings. Who knows best what a taxpayer should save for, the government or the taxpayer? With ***The Best Tax Solution*** lower income tax rate and lower Medicare tax rate will allow taxpayers to decide for themselves their personal saving priorities.

Complexity in the current tax code causes most taxpayers to obtain third party assistance in preparation of tax returns, making them sacrifice their financial liberty to strangers and eventually the government. Your finances should be for your eyes only. Each taxpayer, who has a vote, has 3 clear choices on how to fund the federal government; 1) the current unfair and tedious system of reporting income, expenses, paying excise taxes, and government fees, or 2) an unfair regressive consumption tax (see Chapter 7 – Other Solutions), or 3) ***The Best Tax Solution*** which is simple and fair with a single page tax form.

Social Security Solvency

In 1983 when Social Security was last reformed, the Social Security trustees estimated the trust fund would remain solvent for 75 years, until 2058. Now the trustees estimate that the fund will be insolvent by 2033 without reform. However the Heritage Foundation predicts the fund may become insolvent by 2024. Even now the fund's expenditures on benefits exceed the revenue from payroll taxes, adding to the annual budget deficit. ***The Best Tax Solution*** expands the base of Social Security contributions, thus making Social Security less dependent on wages, and will extend the solvency by at least 50 years without any other reforms. *The New Paradigm – Volume II* will extend solvency in perpetuity and fix the Social Security spending paradigm.

Medicare Solvency

When Medicare solvency is discussed, the Hospital Insurance (HI) trust fund or Part A is the main target. Part A is financed primarily from payroll taxes paid by current workers.   Parts B and D or the Supplementary Medical Insurance trust fund are financed from beneficiary premiums and general revenue, thus making them immune from insolvency, but with high potential impact on budget deficits. The HI trust fund is nothing more than an accounting gimmick, without any transfer of funds, run by the U.S. Treasury. Because the HI trust fund is based on current assets, when the asset balance is less than zero the fund is considered insolvent. There is no provision or law instituted by Congress to pay Part A bills from general revenues. When Part A does become insolvent, only a fraction of hospital bills will be paid. Insolvency has been estimated to be 2030 by the Medicare Trustees, although it fluctuates from year to year based on healthcare costs and wages. The Affordable Care Act (Obamacare) in 2010 miraculously moved the expected insolvency date from 2017 to 2029 (give or take 5 years), through questionable productivity adjustments and increased contributions from the more affluent. In any event, Obamacare pushed the solvency issue past President Obama's term to the detriment of the budget deficit.

Medicaid and its expansion under Obamacare, although not financed with payroll taxes, will double in the Obama administration from $200 billion in 2008 to $400 billion in 2018 for the federal portion, all of which amounts to deficit spending. This 100% increase in costs is accompanied with an increase of less than 50% in enrollment. Only the government could devise a system so inefficient and corrupt, as well as with dubious constitutionality.

The Best Tax Solution expands the base of Medicare contributions, thus making Medicare less dependent on wages, and will extend the solvency by at least 50 years without any other reforms. *The New Paradigm – Volume II* will extend solvency in perpetuity and fix the Medicare spending paradigm and also address the Medicaid dilemma.

Elimination of Internal Revenue Code

No single person, neither in the IRS or outside, can possibly interpret the more than 75,000 pages of the Internal Revenue Code (IRC), although the Title 26 statutes are only a couple of thousand pages. Adding the hundreds of thousands of pages in rulings by the tax court, spawn a system so arcane and complex that fear of noncompliance is rampant and justified. Tentacles in the IRC reach into every aspect of the government and American lives, compelling behavior unproductive for society and interfering with the wants and needs of the American people. *The Best Tax Solution* removes these tentacles that benefit primarily special interest groups and social engineers. Within 2 years this humongous collection of stifling rules and regulations will be replaced by about 100 pages of clear and concise language that does not require a tax attorney or CPA to interpret. The actual statute will be reduced from several thousand pages to less than 10 pages.

Elimination of IRS Workforce

Creating jobs is a stated goal of *The Best Tax Solution*, but with the change in paradigms about 90,000 jobs will be lost at the IRS. Knowledge regarding the IRC will no longer be needed, except for legacy audits and delinquent filings. Early retirement and attrition will account for some 20,000, leaving the remaining employees available for retraining at the bureau of Immigration and Customs Enforcement so desperately in need of border control agents and immigrant processing. Personnel from the 19 tax courts can be reassigned to increase the number of immigration courts from the current 58.

.Within 3 years of passing *The Best Tax Solution* the cost of collecting income taxes, Social Security, and Medicare will drop from $12 billion annually to roughly $2 billion, a not insignificant reduction to the budget deficit. Imagine a life without the constant fear of audit and retribution from the IRS. Imagine IRS not being able to make someone justify whether they are operating a non-profit entity. Imagine IRS not influencing taxpayers into actions some bureaucrat "feels" is best.

Reduction of Tax Professionals

Tax attorneys and accountants will also take a hit in the employment arena. Third party tax preparation firms, such as H&R Block, may cease to exist, like the companies that made buggy whips when the car took over the transportation industry. Tax preparation software will be reduced to state returns until even states adopt the simple solution. Possibly a million unproductive jobs, or 20% of the total, will be lost with *The Best Tax Solution* implementation removing a massive drain on resources that can better be used to bolster economic growth. These leaches on society will fight fiercely to protect their domain, but eventually they will be absorbed into a more vital economy. Imagine not needing a tax attorney to shelter estates from confiscatory federal death tax and securing *"the Blessings of Liberty for ourselves and our Posterity"* as stated in the preamble of the Constitution. Imagine businesses not needing accountants and third-party payroll firms, such as ADP, because of the simplicity of no W2s, no W9s, no depreciation, and no tax credits.

Decrease of People in Poverty

An intended goal of reducing poverty by 5% per year is achieved by removing payroll taxes from the lowest income individuals, setting a livable subsistence level, and eliminating regressive federal excise taxes such as gasoline. Income inequality is perpetuated by regressive federal payroll taxes, regressive government fees, and regressive excise taxes. *The Best Tax Solution* gives an immediate raise of 7.65% to all workers earning less than the minimum subsistence level, putting up to an extra $1,900 in the pockets of the working poor. An incentive will be created for lower income taxpayers to save money by annual refunds of withholding income tax and Medicare, amounting to $3,250 for taxpayers earning the minimum subsistence level. While tax credits will be eliminated, the added benefit of filing separate returns for married couples creates a minimum subsistence level of $50,000 for working families, alleviating the current disincentive to avoid the marriage tax inequity. Savings from regressive gasoline tax, phone tax, and numerous government fees will add another $500 to lower income taxpayers.

Elimination of Excise Taxes

IRS's Publication 510 is the regressive recipe book for excise taxes including everything from fuel taxes of $.184 per gallon of gasoline and $.194 for aviation fuel to the 11% excise tax on bows. Excise taxes make most items cost more, stemming from environmental taxes, communication taxes, air transportation taxes, sport fishing equipment taxes, electric outboard motor tax, coal tax, tire tax, gas guzzler automobile tax, vaccine tax, heavy truck tax, ship passenger tax, foreign insurance tax, indoor tanning services tax, and patient-centered outcomes research fee. Publication 510 does not even cover all the excise taxes, it excludes alcohol tax, tobacco tax, firearm tax, heavy highway vehicle use tax, wagering tax, and occupational tax. Not only do these regressive taxes pose a tremendous burden on society and low income taxpayers by making basic needs more expensive from shipping to energy, but the compliance cost of reporting and tracking is untenable. Did America learn anything from the Great Depression of the 1930s when the majority of federal tax revenue was from regressive excise taxes? *The Best Tax Solution* removes this scourge on the American taxpayer helping the poor and making the United States more competitive globally.

Elimination of Government Fees

What the federal government can not take from taxpayers through taxes, they impose a government fee which Americans are made to believe is for services that are outside the services that citizens are entitled to receive. Oh if it were true, instead of the money grab that it truly has become. If the government should provide a service, then it should be free to all Americans, if not then it should be made available by the private sector. Many of the excise taxes the government charges are actually fees, such as the ship passenger tax, the patient centered outcomes research fee, indoor tanning salon tax, and the heavy highway

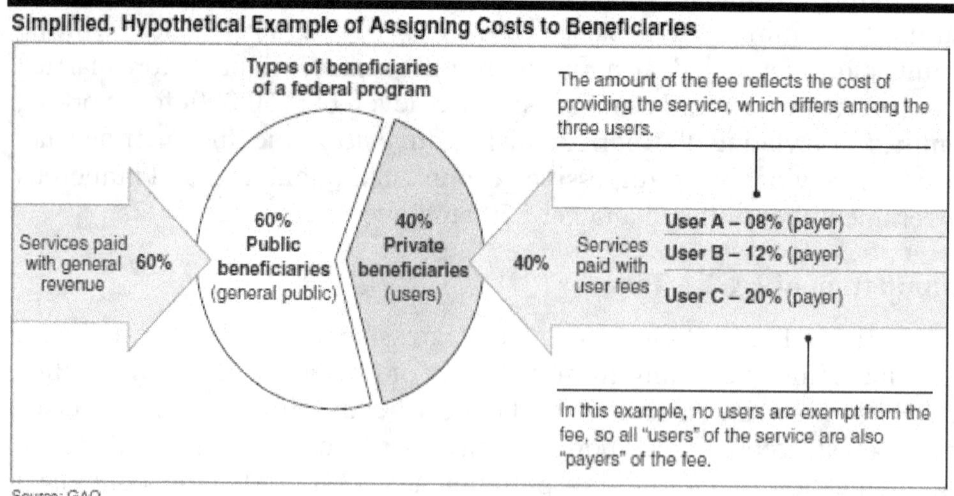

vehicle use tax. Regardless of what they are called, these regressive encumbrances are not fair for services that should be equally available to all.

The Congressional Budget Office (CBO) defines a user fee as "money that the federal government charges for services, or for the sale or use of federal goods or resources, that generally provide benefits to the recipients beyond those that may accrue to the general public. The amount of a user fee is typically related to the cost of the service provided or the value of the good or resource used. . .". A distinction must be made between user fees and other fees that should more appropriately be called insurance, guarantees, or rental charges. Insurance examples crop insurance, flood insurance, and mortgage insurance. Guarantee examples include student loans, direct federal loans, and pension guarantees. Rental charges examples include grazing rights, logging rights, and lease payments for energy exploration/production. A common characteristic to these "non user fees" is that 1) they vary widely based on location, land area, asset value, or loan amount, and 2) they should rightfully belong to the private sector or to the states. The federal government is notorious for circumventing states sovereignty and competing with the private sector.

Are all people entitled to security when they fly commercial airlines? If so, why does TSA charge a security fee? Is everyone entitled to obtain a copyright for their creations? Is everyone entitled to a copy of their tax returns? Is everyone entitled to a replacement Social Security card if it's lost or stolen? Are poor people allowed entrance to National Parks? If all Americans have the freedom to travel internationally and a passport is required, why are not passports free? Is every American allowed to see government information? If so, why is there a fee to obtain information through the Freedom of Information Act (FOIA)? Why not make all non-classified government information available online? Fees everywhere, application fees, regulatory fees, auction fees, forfeiture fees, patent fees, trademark fees, and inspection fees, to name a few.

The Government Accounting Office (GAO) has simplified the process for imposing federal fees by publishing a document titled *"Federal User Fees: A Design Guide"* to assist Congress in confiscating money from innocent Americans. The GAO found that using the "beneficiary pays principle can promote equity and economic efficiency". In actuality it provides cover to gutless politicians to raise extra revenue for their nefarious goals. Based on the theory that people would use fewer government services if they had to pay for the services. Do Americans need more than one passport? Do all Americans need inventions patented or trademarked every day? Do authors publish a book every day? Although the Constitution authorized Congress to build Post Offices and Post Roads, authority to charge postage was granted in the Postal Service Act of 1792. Since the Post Office became a quasi-independent corporation in 1970, *The Best Tax Solution* does not intend to eliminate fees for postage, but all other federal government fees will be placed on the ash heap of history.

Elimination of Duties

United States Customs and Border Protection (CBP) is the agency within the Department of Homeland Security responsible for collecting customs duties. A customs duty is a tariff or tax imposed by countries for goods that cross international borders. While most customs duties are governed by trade agreements, some are in place as protectionist measures to protect the economy, jobs, residents, or environment. The Harmonized Tariff Schedule (HTS), published by the United States International Trade Commission, lists the duty rate and limits for virtually every item that can be brought into the United States. While limits or bans for goods may be necessary to protect the environment, national security, and health, any other limits or bans simply deny Americans lower prices for goods that are not essential or are punitive to other countries. Irrespective of limits or bans, duties should only be imposed on countries that require tariffs on goods the United States exports to them. This includes other countries that charge a value added tax (VAT) or tariffs on imports. Free trade is one thing, stupid trade is another. *The Best Tax Solution* over time will eliminate all duties for trading partners that reciprocate. In the meantime, duties on goods brought home by Americans traveling internationally will cease immediately after implementation, because it's just too petty.

Increased Domestic Energy Production

Imported oil, not exported as finished goods, will be taxed more heavily than oil drilled in the United States. For example, oil from Saudi Arabia will be taxed by *The Best Tax Solution* as income for the difference between what it cost at the wellhead to the price when it arrives at a United States refinery, because shipping costs of international goods and commodities are not deductible. If a barrel of oil costs $10 a barrel to pump from Saudi Arabia and it costs an American refiner $50 a barrel, income tax, Social Security, and Medicare, totaling 18% will be charged on the $40 a barrel of income. If a like barrel of oil arrives from an American oilfield, the income is the cost to pump the oil and the cost of shipping to the refinery, making domestic oil production more financially acceptable.

Repeal of 16th Amendment

Progressives, both Democrats and Republicans, proposed and ratified the 16th Amendment in 1913, to ostensibly make everyone pay their "fair share" and "soak the rich". Boy, that sure didn't work, now nobody pays their fair share and every taxpayer is soaked. Not only did the 16th Amendment not work, it circumvented other rights guaranteed in the Constitution, not the least of which are the 4th and 14th Amendments. Privacy rights granted in the 4th Amendment which states in part; *"The right of the people to be secure in their persons, houses, papers, and effects, against unreasonable searches and seizures, shall not be violated..."*, are constantly trashed by the IRS when performing audits. Since the IRS only audits 2% of income tax returns and progressive taxation by definition does not provide equal protection as guaranteed in the 14th Amendment, IRS denies due process and equal protection because IRS rules through regulation and not the law.

Chapter 5 - Scenarios Using The Best Tax Solution

Every person and every other entity is unique in their purpose and goals, as is their right. Being unique does not mean they are entitled to their own tax methodology. Unique tax methodologies are the epitome of special interest and unfairness. Any provision in the tax code that advantages one entity does so to the detriment of all others.

This chapter will show various scenarios of how entities are treated in the current tax code and how ***The Best Tax Solution*** treats the same taxpayer. In several cases the current tax code will have no tax liability and ***The Best Tax Solution*** will have a tax liability, always in the interest of fairness. In all cases ***The Best Tax Solution*** will be fair to all taxpayers, where the current tax code is not. The tax base is greatly expanded so that corporations like General Electric that earned $14,000,000,000.00 in 2010 and paid no taxes, to the detriment of all others, can no longer game the system.

Under the current tax system the Social Security portion of the payroll tax, also known as FICA, was temporarily reduced to 5.2% from 6.2% for 2011 and 2012. The political class temporarily lowered this to "stimulate" the economy, or in reality to get reelected. In all the scenarios shown below the real rate of 6.2% for Social Security and 1.45% for Medicare, a total of 7.65%, is used. Currently the Social Security portion is only paid on the first $118,500 of wages whereas Medicare has no upper limit. The employer matches FICA withheld from the employee. In contrast, ***The Best Tax Solution*** only has a payroll tax of 3.0% to all taxpayers for Medicare.

Scenarios will show not only the impact on the individual taxpayer, but the employer and government as well. What will be demonstrated is that ***The Best Tax Solution*** treats all taxpayers equally and is easy to implement. The scenarios exclude unemployment insurance and disability insurance since these vary for each state. For example, unemployment insurance has a federal and a state component and applies to only a portion of wages, to the detriment of the lower paid individual. Unemployment insurance is a very regressive tax, as far as taxes go because they impact only lower income taxpayers in volatile jobs.

Following are 16 different taxable scenarios which encompass most individuals and entities in the country. For each scenario, the premise, the tax liability under the current tax code, the same under *The Best Tax Solution*, and the reasons why *The Best Tax Solution* is superior in every scenario. It might be helpful if readers refer to Chapter 1 of this book for the components of *The Best Tax Solution*.

Taxpayer Profile	Gross Income	Current Tax and FICA	Best Tax and FICA[5]	Difference
Poor	$14,500	$1,109.25	$0	$1,109.25
Very Poor	$25,000	$1,912.50	$0	$1,912.50
Lucky	$48,600	$3,548	$3,068	$480
Unlucky	$20,000	$0	$0	$0
Wanna Be	$60,000	$4,781	$4,550	$231
Middle Class	$60,000	$4,781	$4,160	$621
Dinks	$90,000	$11,164	$9,652.50	$1,511.50
Sheppies	$451,000	$13,521	$52,130	($38,609)
Rich	$15.7 M	$2,697,119	$3,410,025	($712,906)
Ultra Rich	$325 M	$20 M[6]	$58.5 M	($38.5 M)
Small Business	$250,000[7]	$63,430	$40,500	$22,930
Medium Biz	$20 M	$100,000	$2.812 M	($2.712 M)
Conglomerate	$150 B	$1 B	$10.65 B	($9.65 B)
Large Non-Profit	$500 M	($4 M)	$90 M	($94 M)
Small Non-Profit	$10,000	$0	$500	($500)
Trust Fund	$8 M	$0	$1,440,000	($1,440,000)

---

5   *The Best Tax Solution* only charges the individual for Medicare on income from employers over $25,000.
6   Income Tax Only
7   IRS allows a deduction of $50,000 for overhead that *The Best Tax Solution* does not.

Scenario #1: Single Person at the Poverty Level - "Poor"

Poor

This taxpayer makes the federal minimum wage of $7.25 per hour and works 2,000 hours a year. Their gross income of $14,500 per year comes on 50 weeks of 40 hours per week. This taxpayer is 20 years old and covered by their parent's healthcare.

Under the current tax code:

In the current tax code they will pay $1,109.25 per year in payroll taxes (FICA) leaving them $13,390.75 at the end of the year. They will not get any of the $1,109.25 in payroll taxes back until they retire, if they live long enough.

Under *The Best Tax Solution*:

With *The Best Tax Solution* this taxpayer still earns $14,500 but their payroll tax is $0 because they didn't make $25,000. With the 10% income tax and the 3% for Medicare, this taxpayer will have withheld $1,885, $1,450 in income tax and $435 in Medicare withholding during the year for a total of $1,885. The entire $1,885 withheld will be refunded in February leaving <u>$14,500 at the end of the year</u>. This leaves more for the year, and a refund check for $1,885 that they can save or invest.

The employer will also benefit by paying $725 for Social Security instead of $1,109.25 for Social Security and Medicare. This is especially crucial for small businesses and may indeed create more employment opportunities or allow more profit on which they will pay taxes.

Although this will cost the government $1,109.25 that would have been paid in FICA and $384.25 the employer would have paid for FICA (totaling $1,493.50), the cost should more than be offset by additional spending power to the individual, higher taxable income by the employer, and a reduction of welfare benefits that might otherwise have been paid.

Scenario #2: Working Single Parent - "Very Poor"

This taxpayer has a salary of $25,000 per year. The only benefit they have is 5 paid sick days, otherwise no benefits of any kind. They have two weeks non-paid vacation a year. Two children are in preschool programs and 2 children attend public schools. This taxpayer receives annual welfare benefits of $19,000, $4,000 in food assistance, $6,000 in housing allowance, and $9,000 healthcare provided by federal, state, and local governments.

Under the current tax code:
On their $25,000 of income, they pay $1,912.50, netting $23,087.50.

Under *The Best Tax Solution*:
With *The Best Tax Solution* they receive the entire $25,000 (because they do not make more than $25,000 per year), saving $1,912.50.

The employer will also benefit by paying $1,250 for Social Security instead of $1,912.50 for Social Security and Medicare, leaving $662.50 to hire more help or pay more taxes.

Although this will cost the government $1,912.50 that this person would have paid in FICA and $662.50 the employer would have paid for FICA (totaling $2,575), the cost should be offset by higher taxable income by the employer, raises, and a reduction of welfare benefits this person might otherwise receive.

Scenario #3: Fixed Income Retiree - "Lucky"

This person makes $20,000 per year in Social Security benefits and $25,000 per year in a pension plan, for a total of $45,000. Additionally their retirement plan provides $3,600 for their Medicare premium payments.

Under the current tax code:
With the current tax code this taxpayer pays $3,548, all of which is income tax.

Under *The Best Tax Solution*:
With *The Best Tax Solution* the yearly amount is $3,068 (($48,600 - $25,000) * 0.13), $2,360 for income tax, $0 for Social Security, and $708 for Medicare. The *The Best Tax Solution* treats any retirement income as it would any other investment income.

The trust fund paying the pension benefits would withhold 13% for income tax ($2,360) and Medicare ($708) on the $23,600 ($48,600 - $25,000), or $3,068. The higher the pension and Social Security benefits the more this "Lucky" person would pay the government. No Social Security is paid because the taxpayer is collecting Social Security.

The new revenue to the federal government would be a decrease of $480.

Scenario #4: Fixed Income Retiree - "Unlucky"

This person makes $20,000 per year in Social Security benefits.

(Under the current tax code and ***The Best Tax Solution***) No employer or government revenue would be affected for this "Unlucky" person.

Scenario #5: Married Single Income with Kids - "Wanna be Middle Class"

This couple has 3 young children at home with the non-working spouse. The working spouse has a salary of $60,000 per year without healthcare benefits for which they pay a premium of $12,000 per year. They own a home with a monthly mortgage of $2,000. Because of mortgage and healthcare premiums they have only $19,219 of disposable income for food, clothing, and all other incidentals.

Under the current tax code:
With the current tax code this taxpayer pays $4,781, $191 of which is income tax and $4,590 for FICA.

Under ***The Best Tax Solution***:
With ***The Best Tax Solution*** they do slightly better with disposable income of $19,450.

The employer currently pays $4,590 in payroll taxes (FICA). With ***The Best Tax Solution*** the employer would pay $3,000 for Social Security, a savings of $1,590.

Although this will cost the government $231 that this person would have paid in FICA and $1,590 the employer would have paid for FICA (totaling $1,821), the cost should more than be offset by higher taxable income by the employer and a reduction of welfare benefits this couple might otherwise receive.

Scenario #6: Double Income with Kids - "Middle Class"

This family has 3 children in public school and one spouse making a salary of $30,000 per year with full benefits, including healthcare which the employer pays $12,000 per year and a retirement plan. Currently her employer puts $10,000 a year into a 401K retirement plan. The other spouse is an employee earning $30 per hour and working about 1,000 hours, earning $30,000. They own a home with a monthly mortgage of $2,000.

Under the current tax code:
After income tax of $191 and FICA of $4,590 they net $55,179. Because of the mortgage they have $31,179 of disposable income for food, clothing, and all other incidentals.

Under ***The Best Tax Solution***:
With ***The Best Tax Solution*** they do slightly better with net income of $55,840 (($30,000 - $25,000 + $12,000 + $10,000) * 0.13) + (($30,000 - $25,000) * 0.13) disposable income of $31,840.

The employer currently pays $4,590 in payroll taxes (FICA). With ***The Best Tax Solution*** the employer would pay $3,000 for Social Security, a savings of $1,590.

Although this will cost the government $621 that this couple would have paid in income tax and FICA and $1,590 the employer would have paid for FICA (totaling $2,211), the cost should more than be offset by higher taxable income by the employer and a reduction of welfare benefits, such as child care, this couple might otherwise receive.

Scenario #7: Double Income No Kids - "Dinks"

This couple has no children and one spouse making a salary of $30,000 per year with healthcare benefit which the employer pays $8,000 per year. The other spouse is a union member earning $40 per hour and working 1,500 hours, grossing $60,000 per year. This spouse pays union dues of $55 per month and a work assessment dues of $2 per hour worked (total dues for 1,500 hours is $3,660). This spouse has a pension plan (defined benefit) and a 401k (defined contribution) with the employer paying $2 per hour into the 401k and $7.50 per hour into the pension plan. This spouse's employer pays $8 per hour for full benefit healthcare (total benefits for 1,500 hours is $26,250). The couple had deductions totaling $55,310 leaving a taxable income of $34,690.

<u>Under the current tax code:</u>
Their income tax came to $4,279 and FICA was $6,885 (totaling $11,164). Since they are married and file jointly, the FICA for one is $2,295 and $4,590 for the other.

<u>Under *The Best Tax Solution*</u>:
With *The Best Tax Solution* they file separately and their total is slightly less at $9,652.50, $1,690 (($38,000-$25,000)*0.13) for one and $7,962.50 (($60,000-$25,000+$26,250)*0.13) for the other.

The employers currently pay $6,885 in payroll taxes (FICA). With *The Best Tax Solution* the employers would pay $6,212.50 (($30,000 + $8,000 + $60,000 +$26,250) * 0.05) for Social Security, a savings of $672.50.

Although this will cost the government $1,511.50 that this couple would have paid in income tax and FICA and $672.50 the employers would have paid for FICA (totaling $2,184), the cost should more than be offset by higher taxable income by the employers and a reduction of welfare benefits, such as child care, this couple might otherwise receive.

Scenario #8: *Suburban Hi-tech Educated Professional - "Sheppies"*

This taxpayer is a computer professional earning $150,000 per year for a Fortune 500 company, including healthcare and a 401k plan. The employer pays $16,000 per year for the health plan and matches the $10,000 per year this person puts in the 401k. The spouse is a doctor earning $200,000 per year in a private practice and contributes 10% of his income to an IRA and another 10% to church. They own a beautiful house with a mortgage of $5,000 per month and numerous expenses for business purposes, health savings account, and college tuition for their 2 children. They jointly made $10,000 in interest, $20,000 in dividends, and $35,000 in capital gains. Because of business write-offs, personal deductions, and adjustments they paid a total of $13,521 of which $13,322 was FICA ($7,347 for Social Security and $5,975 for Medicare) and $199 income tax for overpayment to their health savings account.

<u>Under the current tax code:</u>
They paid **zero** dollars in income tax on total income of $451,000, excluding the early distribution penalty of $199.

<u>Under *The Best Tax Solution*</u>:
With *The Best Tax Solution* they will pay $52,130 (($451,000 - $50,000) * 0.13) of which $40,100 is income tax and $12,030 for Medicare.

The employers currently pay $12,422 for FICA ($7,347 for Social Security and $5,075 for Medicare) on wages of $350,000. Additionally, the brokers that handled their investment income of $65,000 deducted nothing. With *The Best Tax Solution* the employers would pay $19,300 ($386,000 * 0.05) for Social Security and their broker would withhold $3,250 ($65,000 * 0.05) for Social Security on their investment income. This totals $22,550 withheld for Social Security.

With the current tax code the total revenue to the federal government is $41,177, $199 for income tax, $29,928 for Social Security, and $11,050 for Medicare. With *The Best Tax Solution* total revenue to the federal government would be $74,680, $40,100 for income tax,

$22,550 for Social Security, and $12,030 for Medicare. This would be an increase of $33,503. It's no wonder why there's income inequality.

Scenario #9: Highly Paid Executive or Personality - "Rich"

This taxpayer has a personal employment contract valued at $6,000,000 per year, excluding of an assortment of benefits. This person is very socially conscious and donates $3,000,000 to charities. This person has numerous deductions, write-offs, and expenses totaling $6,369,515 including the $3,000,000 to charities.

Under the current tax code:
They paid a total of $2,602,772, $2,456,675 for income tax, $7,347 for Social Security, and $138,750 for Medicare.

Under *The Best Tax Solution*:
With *The Best Tax Solution* they would have paid $3,410,025, $2,027,500 for income tax, $1,013,750 for Social Security, and $369,775 for Medicare.

The employer currently pays $94,347 for FICA ($7,347 for Social Security and $87,000 for Medicare) on wages of $6,000,000. Additionally, the brokers that handled their investment income of $9,700,000 deducted nothing. With *The Best Tax Solution* the employer would pay $19,300 ($386,000 * 0.05) for Social Security and their broker would withhold $3,250 ($65,000 * 0.05) for Social Security on their investment income. This totals $22,550 withheld for Social Security.

With the current tax code the total revenue to the federal government is $41,177, $199 for income tax, $29,928 for Social Security, and $11,050 for Medicare. With *The Best Tax Solution* total revenue to the federal government would be $74,680, $40,100 for income tax, $22,550 for Social Security, and $12,030 for Medicare. This would be an increase of $33,503. It's no wonder why there's income inequality.

Scenario #10: Investor - "Ultra Rich"

This taxpayer earns in excess of $325,000,000 per year exclusively from capital gains, interest, dividends, and business income.

<u>Under the current tax code:</u>
Because of write offs, business expenses, mortgage deductions, and a plethora of tax breaks, the taxpayer is left with a meager $38,794,940 in taxable income. On this income of $38,794,940 this taxpayer pays $20,246,330 believing it's more than their fair-share, when it's actually only 6.22%, certainly less than their secretaries. Not a penny of this $20,246,330 goes to Social Security or Medicare.

<u>Under **The Best Tax Solution**</u>:
With **The Best Tax Solution** this taxpayer would pay $58,500,000, $32,500,000 for income tax, $16,250,000 for Social Security, and $9,750,000 for Medicare. Since $235,000,000 of the $325,000,000 was investment income, the brokers, banks, and other entities would withhold $42,300,000, $23,500,000 for income taxes, $11,750,000 for Social Security, and $7,050,000 for Medicare.

Scenario #11: Small Business

This taxpayer has 15 employees and revenue of $1,000,000 per year. The total payroll with all salaries, benefits, and FICA is $500,000. The cost of goods amounts to $250,000 and another $50,000 is spent on facilities and other overhead, leaving $200,000 for the owner that is taken as personal income because the company qualifies as a sub-chapter S corporation.

<u>Under the current tax code:</u>
On the $200,000, this small business pays $63,430, $43,380 for income tax and $20,050 in self-employment tax ($14,508 for Social Security and $5,542 for Medicare).

<u>Under **The Best Tax Solution**</u>:
With **The Best Tax Solution** this taxpayer would have paid $40,500, $22,500 for income tax, $11,250 for Social Security, and $6,750 for Medicare. With the extra $22,930 this small business may give raises, hire a new worker, or expand.

While the government has reduced revenue from small businesses, additional revenue is generated for Medicare which is most in need of funds. Lower taxes on small businesses will cause more small businesses to be formed compared to the current stagnation and failures of small businesses.

Scenario #12: Medium Business

This taxpayer has 500 employees, 100 in the United States, and world-wide revenue of $20,000,000 per year, $15,000,000 in the United States. This company manufacturers high-tech widgets, exclusively overseas. Their cost of goods is $6,000,000 per year ($4,000,000 for labor, $1,900,000 for components, and $100,000 for raw materials) of all of which is spent outside the United States. Their cost of sales is low at $1,000,000 per year because they use third party distributors and have only a handful of direct sales offices in the United States. They pay their executives and administrative staff extremely well to the tune of $2,000,000 a year. Additional expenses and write-offs total $4,000,000 leaving pretax earnings of $7,000,000 of which they leave $6,000,000 outside the United States, repatriating a mere $1,000,000. They pay dividends of $500,000 each year and foreign taxes of $500,000.

Under the current tax code:
Because of creative accounting, they pay a paltry $100,000 in income tax and nothing for Social Security or Medicare, except what they pay in FICA for their 100 employees in the United States.

Under ***The Best Tax Solution***:
With ***The Best Tax Solution*** they would pay $2,812,000, $1,340,000 in income tax, $920,000 in Social Security, and $552,000 in Medicare. Domestic income is $13,500,000, which is $15,000,000 revenue less $1,000,000 in domestic cost-of-sales less $500,000 in dividends paid. Taxes on domestic sales would be $2,430,000, $1,350,000 for income tax, $675,000 for Social Security, and $405,000 for Medicare. International income is $4,900,000, $5,000,000 revenue less $100,000 in raw materials. Their taxes on international sales would be $382,000 (reduced by $500,000 paid in foreign taxes), a negative $10,000 in income taxes, $245,000 in Social Security, and $147,000 in Medicare.

If this same company manufactured their widgets in the United States they would pay $1,710,000 with ***The Best Tax Solution***, a savings of $1,102,000. Their domestic income would be $7,500,000 ($15,000,000 - $6,000,000 - $1,000,000 - $500,000) creating a tax obligation of $1,350,000, $750,000 in income tax, $375,000 in Social Security, and $225,000 in Medicare. Their international income would be $4,500,000 ($5,000,000 - $500,000) of which they pay $360,000, $0 for income tax, $225,000 for Social Security, and $135,000 for Medicare. Additional savings will come from shipping costs, tax attorneys, and accountants, greatly reducing administrative overhead.

With ***The Best Tax Solution*** the federal government revenues would increase by $2,712,000, $1,240,000 in income tax, $920,000 in Social Security, and $552,000 in Medicare. If this company would change their business model and manufacture in the United States, hundreds of jobs would be created.

Scenario #13: Large Multinational Conglomerate

This taxpayer has over 300,000 employees, 125,000 in the United States, and world-wide revenue of $150,000,000,000 per year, $75,000,000,000 in the United States. This company has 8 business segments that include manufacturing, financial services, and construction. Their COGS is $75,000,000,000 per year, $50,000,000,000 ($2,000,000,000 in raw materials) of which is spent outside the United States. Their COS is $17,000,000,000 per year, $7,000,000,000 in the United States. Half of the products and services made in the United States are exported and half of the products and services made overseas are imported. They pay their executives and administrative staff extremely well to the tune of $4,000,000,000 a year.

Under the current tax code:
Additional (Current tax code allowable) expenses and write-offs total $22,000,000,000 leaving pretax earnings of $15,000,000,000 of which they leave $12,000,000,000 outside the United States, repatriating a mere $3,000,000,000. They pay dividends of $3,000,000,000 each year and foreign taxes of $1,000,000,000. Because of creative accounting, they pay a paltry $1,000,000,000 in income tax and nothing for Social Security or Medicare, except what they pay in FICA for their 125,000 employees in the United States.

Under *The Best Tax Solution*:
With *The Best Tax Solution* they would pay $10.65 B, $4.25 B in income tax, $4 B in Social Security, and $2.4 B in Medicare. Domestic income is $52.5 B, which is $75 B revenue less $12.5 B (half of domestic COGS) less $7 B in domestic COS less $3 B in dividends paid. Taxes on domestic sales would be $9.45 B, $5.25 B for income tax, $2.625 B for Social Security, and $1.575 B for Medicare. International income is $27.5 B, $75 B revenue less $37.5 B (half of domestic COGS and half of international COGS) in COGS less $10 B in COS. Their taxes on international sales would be $1.2 B (reduced by $1 B paid in foreign taxes), a negative $1 B in income taxes, $1.375 B in Social Security, and $825 M in Medicare.

With *The Best Tax Solution* the federal government revenues would be $10.65 B, $4.25 B in income tax, $4 B in Social Security, and $2.4 B in Medicare. If this company would change their business model and manufacture in the United States, thousands of jobs would be created and taxes paid would be reduced by approximately $3 B.

Scenario #14: Large Non-profit Entity

This taxpayer, an actual nonprofit, is organized into no fewer than ten entities, including a 501(c)(4)[1], several 501(c)(3)[2]s, a 509(a)(1)[3], a grantor trust[4], a wholly owned taxable subsidiary, and various taxable special purpose affiliates. The organization is formed as a 501(c)(4) with a wholly owned taxable subsidiary providing services to the organization and its affiliates. This service entity receives fees from the parent for providing service, third party consulting revenues, and a no fee license to use the parent company's trademarks and service marks. An affiliated foundation, a 501(c)(3) and a 509(a)(1), that receives money principally from the federal government, the parent company, corporations, and individuals. The foundation has an affiliated institute that is also a 501(c)(3) undoubtedly for collection of funds not appropriate for a public charity. Another 501(c)(3) corporation provides free legal assistance and education with contributions from the parent, government grants, other foundations, corporations, and individuals. A grantor trust was established for members or the general benefit of the parent. This trust is funded by premiums from members. The trust pays the parent company a royalty and then pays third party providers a negotiated amount for member premiums. Where the excess premiums end up is a mystery to this day. Another 501(c)(3) was formed to engage people in community service and leadership activities. Funding is from federal grants and contributions from the parent. Another affiliated LLC was formed with the parent as the sole member in order to provide a self-funding mechanism for the deductible portion of insurance coverage with third-party administrators.

This nonprofit conglomerate has about 2,000 employees, 37,000,000 members, and more than 1,200 local chapters that are operated as separate entities. In 2014, excluding local chapters, the corporation reported operating revenues of almost $1.5 B. The revenue came from royalties ($799 M – 54% from the grantor trust), membership dues ($296 M), publications ($146 M), grants ($92 M), contributions ($89

---

1   501(c)(4) organizations are civic leagues or associations operated exclusively for the promotion of social welfare or local associations of employees with limited membership.

2   501(c)(3) organizations are either a public charity, private foundation or private operating foundation with open membership

3   509(a)(1) organizations are deemed a public charity

4   Grantor trusts are a tax loophole so no taxes are paid by a trust fund

M), program income ($58 M), and miscellaneous of ($6 M). Additionally, non-operating investment income of $97 M was reported, of which $26 M was generated from the grantor trust. The grantor trust processed $9 B in premium payments from insured members. The premium payments to *"insurance carriers are classified as agency transactions, and, as such, are not recorded as either revenue or expenses"*.

Under the current tax code:
On the nearly $10.6 B in income (described in this scenario), they (this corporation) claimed a tax credit of more than $4 M.

Direct operating expenses reported were slightly more than $1 B, $425 M in programs and field services, $188 M in publications, $371 M in member services, and $66 M in research and other. Indirect supporting services reported were $418 M, $165 M for membership development and $253 M for management and other. Assuming the grantor trust had **zero** net revenue after paying royalties and insurance premiums (a big assumption) and without scrutinizing the expenses, the operating income was nearly $500 M.

Under ***The Best Tax Solution***:
With ***The Best Tax Solution*** the tax liability for this nonprofit scam would be a minimum of $90 M ($500 M * 0.18), $50 M for income tax, $25 M for Social Security, and $15 M for Medicare. Not only does this nonprofit receive tens of millions of dollars in grants from the federal government, they spend around $100 M in lobbying for more beneficial treatment and their social engineering goals, to the detriment of their members and the American people.

Scenario #15: Small Non-profit Entity

This taxpayer, a medium sized church, <u>currently pays no taxes</u> (receives) <u>on</u> $1,000,000 (annually) from gifts and donations. Also, the church earns $10,000 annually in investment income.

<u>Under the current tax code:</u>
(This taxpayer currently pays no taxes)

<u>Under **The Best Tax Solution**</u>:
With **The Best Tax Solution** the church would pay $500 on their investment income, all of which will go to Social Security because they do not reach the subsistence income level for income tax and Medicare. In exchange, the church would be freed from the "Johnson Amendment[1]"

---

1   The 1954 Johnson Amendment prevents non-profit organizations from advocating political viewpoints.

Scenario #16: Trust Funds

This taxpayer is a multi-employer defined benefit pension plan with 15 employers, 1,000 active members, and 500 retirees. The fund has assets of $100,000,000 invested in various financial instruments. All contributions to the plan are made by the employers and total $5,000,000 annually. Benefits paid to retirees come to $2,000,000 a year. The return on investments adds an additional $7,000,000 each year, $3,000,000 in dividends, $1,000,000 in interest and $3,000,000 in capital gains. Of the $3,000,000 in capital gains, the fund had gains of $4,000,000 on 50 transactions and losses of $1,000,000 on 10 transactions. Expenses for the plan are $900,000 for brokers, insurance, consultants, attorneys, and accountants. An extra $100,000 is spent for the obligatory meeting in Hawaii for the trustees and consultants. Currently the employers deduct the $5,000,000 in contributions and no employer or member pays any taxes on the contributions. The retirees may or may not have income tax withheld from their benefit checks and no money is withheld for Social Security or Medicare.

Under the current tax code:
No taxes of any kind are paid by the fund on their investment income.

Under ***The Best Tax Solution***:
With ***The Best Tax Solution*** the employers would no longer be able to deduct the $5,000,000 they make in contributions, taxes would be paid on investment income, and retirees would have taxes withheld for income tax, Social Security, and Medicare. On the investment income of $8,000,000 ($3,000,000 dividends, $1,000,000 interest, and $4,000,000 capital gains) the fund would pay $1,440,000, $800,000 for income taxes, $400,000 for Social Security, and $240,000 for Medicare. The retirees would have $360,000 withheld on their $2,000,000 in benefits, most of which they will get back when they file their individual return.

Conclusion

In each and every scenario, ***The Best Tax Solution*** is much more simple and fair to the taxpayers of this country compared to the current tax code.

Chapter 6 - Implementing The Best Tax Solution

Many factors go into making ***The Best Tax Solution*** a reality. Foremost of these is convincing the American public, and then the politicians that the current tax code is broken and must be replaced. That should be a very easy task given the state of the current tax code and members of both major political parties favoring tax reform. Next, most taxpayers must be convinced that ***The Best Tax Solution*** is the most likely plan to succeed, and it will make the lives of taxpayers better. After being passed by Congress and signed by the President the work begins on implementing ***The Best Tax Solution***.

A tax reform plan is lacking, if it is not accompanied with a strategy for its implementation. There must first be a strategy for getting it passed, then a strategy for converting the current tax code into the new tax code, and finally a strategy for the ongoing administration of the tax plan. Strategies and mechanics for all of these parts are discussed in summary in this chapter.

Getting the plan passed involves informing the taxpayer, overcoming opposition, pressuring Congress, and convincing the President. Any one of these could be a daunting task that requires a plan and a strategy of its own. This book is the first step in the process of informing the American people about ***The Best Tax Solution***. Overcoming opposition will be the most difficult part of the process. So many people will lose power, millions will lose jobs. Others will lose influence, many will have to pay more in taxes. Lobbyists will be affected as will tax attorneys, accountants, IRS employees, and numerous other government employees. Justifications will be made to the American public to overcome this opposition. Likewise there other tax plans that are being pushed by sometimes well meaning sponsors, in many cases their ego is tied to their plan. Once millions of American taxpayers are convinced that this tax plan is in the best interest of the United States economy and personal liberty, pressuring Congress will be the least difficult step in the process. Finally, the President will sign the bill, if she/he is interested in reelection.

After ***The Best Tax Solution*** is passed, the gargantuan task of transition to the new plan begins in earnest. There are many legacy items in the current tax code that will linger for years, but implementation can commence immediately. A phased implementation will be the least disruptive and will start providing promised benefits within the first year. First to go will be those pesky government user fees and federal excise taxes. Also in the first year, taxpayers will establish their taxpayer profile and familiarize themselves with communicating with the income system. Most of the first year will be spent acquiring the hardware and software to run *The Best Tax Solution* and training personnel to administer the system. Loss of revenue from excise taxes and government fees will be offset by raising the cap on Social Security contributions from employers, imposing a 5% Social Security tax on capital gains, and eliminating loss carry-forwards. This will only last one year, until the remaining features of *The Best Tax Solution* are in place. If all the hardware and software are fully debugged, the second year will see the beginning of full implementation, less legacy items that can not be implemented because of statute or existing trade deals.

Three years after implementation the final audits of the IRS will be completed and the vestiges of the tax code and IRS will become a distant memory. By then the states will be well underway in the repeal of the 16th Amendment

Getting The Best Tax Solution Passed

Convincing the American public that tax reform is needed is not going to be a difficult problem. Getting a critical mass of taxpayers to support *The Best Tax Solution* will be the challenge. Taxpayers will be sold first that tax reform is needed, second that the tax reform must be fair, third that tax reform must be simple, fourth that tax reform is indeed doable, and finally that *The Best Tax Solution* is the only vehicle that can bring it to fruition. During the process of convincing the citizenry, fierce opposition will be thrown in by some anticipated sources and some unanticipated sources. Contingency plans are outlined below for several anticipated opposition efforts and strategic plans will be quickly developed to address unanticipated opposition. Pressuring the Congress and convincing the President will come quite easily once millions of voters are on board.

Convincing the American Public

Educating the American voter will be a major factor along the path to successfully fixing the current dysfunctional income tax, Social Security, and Medicare revenue systems. Other factors include overcoming apathy, organizing concerned citizens, garnering support from high profile individuals, coercing the media into adopting the cause, and having other socially conscience organizations promote the goal. Americans will join the bandwagon either for logical reasons or emotional reasons. Some will join because of hatred for the IRS, some for religious liberty from the Johnson amendment, some for their personal financial well-being, some for personal liberty from government overreach, and some because a friend or relative told them it was a good idea. Strategies will target each of these demographics to ensure a thorough penetration of the electorate.

Education begins with the publication of this book in all available formats including hardcover, paperback, e-book, and audio book. All of the profits from this book will go towards creating a non-profit 501(c)(3) (the current tax code must be utilized in order to replace it, in lieu of anarchy) to educate the electorate, a non-profit 501(c)(4) to promote the passage of *The Best Tax Solution*, and create a website to organize the campaign.

Concerned taxpayers will volunteer to spread the word, sell books, organize speeches to like-minded organizations, conduct surveys, lobby politicians, and circulate petitions. Efforts will be made to attract high profile economists, politicians, and media to further the cause. A website will be developed to help organize volunteers, disseminate information, sell books, conduct surveys, and organize petitions.

Are you a concerned taxpayer? Are you willing to fight with the establishment to improve the country? Initial human resources needed include social media coordinators, web developers, lawyers, promoters, and fundraisers. Eventually these will come with compensation based upon results. If you are interested in exploring this opportunity send an email to admin@thenewparadigmsolutions.com with skills you are willing to contribute or offer for a fee.

The New Paradigm Books

The purpose of this book and series of books is to improve the condition of the United States by educating the American public, proposing workable solutions to problems facing the country, and implementing the solutions to the betterment of the citizenry. The goals of *The New Paradigm: Volume I* are described briefly in the previous chapter and are designed to fix a major scourge on society, namely the IRS and and pending insolvency of Social Security and Medicare. Policies and procedures, hence values, follow the Constitution and are consistent with limited government and personal liberty. Each book in the series gives big-picture strategies and some micro-strategies that will achieve the goals. Human resources necessary to carry out the strategies are summarized for each goal. As the plan is put into operation, numerical evaluations will measure success of the plan and provide analytics to constantly innovate strategies to handle changes encountered.

The New Paradigm: Volume II will advance the solutions required to fix the federal government's spending problems, including entitlements. *Volume II* will concentrate on spending that is not authorized in the Constitution, focusing on limited government and elimination of "investment", the purview of the private sector. Whole departments are put on the chopping block, as well as trimming and consolidation of other departments.

The New Paradigm Group will be formed as a non-profit for the purpose of educating the public, organized under Section 501(c)(3) of Title 26 – Internal Revenue Code. *The New Paradigm Group* is currently staffing with management, writers, editors, business consultants, fund raisers, accountants, clerical personnel, and political "junkies". All of these positions are at home, non-employee, and part-time. Interested persons can send an email to <u>admin@thenewparadigmsolutions.com</u>. If you can't work on your own with minimal direction, don't bother. Keep in mind this is a non-profit corporation, so if you require immediate income, don't bother.

The New Paradigm Non-Profits

Using the tax code in order to repeal and replace it is a core part of the strategy to make **The Best Tax Solution** the law of the land. Many people are familiar with provision of the tax code that allow corporations to operate as a non-profit for the purpose of educating the public, organized under Section 501(c)(3) of Title 26 – Internal Revenue Code. Fewer are aware of the provision of the tax code that allow corporations to operate as a non-profit for the purpose promoting social welfare, organized under Section 501(c)(4) of Title 26 – Internal Revenue Code. Most people are not aware that besides paragraphs (c)(3) and (c)(4) there are more than 25 such paragraphs allowing for non-profit organizations. All of them will disappear, along with rest of the tax code, when **The Best Tax Solution** takes effect.

In addition to *The New Paradigm Group*, *The New Paradigm Foundation* will be formed as a Section 501(c)(3) to educate the public about the federal government's insatiable appetite to control the citizenry through obtrusive tax policy and extra-constitutional manipulation. Additionally, *The New Paradigm Association* will be formed as a Section 501(c)(4) to influence social welfare by lobbying for legislation to fix social ills, litigating to confront unconstitutional power grabs, and organizing efforts to coalesce like minded individuals. Both corporations will be incorporated in Nevada.

The *The New Paradigm Foundation* and *The New Paradigm*

Association are currently staffing with management, attorneys, business consultants, fund raisers, accountants, and clerical personnel. All of these positions are at home, non-employee, and part-time. Interested persons can send an email to admin@thenewparadigmsolutions.com. If you can't work on your own with minimal direction, don't bother. Keep in mind these are non-profit corporations, so if you require immediate income, don't bother.

The New Paradigm Website

Technology and social media will make *The Best Tax Solution* a reality and will play an integral part of organizing the effort to educate taxpayers, overcome political opposition, and ultimately implementing *The Best Tax Solution*. Features will 1) allow staff and volunteers to coordinate efforts to convince taxpayers and politicians of the solutions envisioned in The New Paradigm series of books, books, and audio books, 2) provide a forum for various ideas on improving proposed solutions and novel methods for fixing the country's problems, 3) establish a conduit for fund raising and sale of books and other materials to further the purpose, and 4) conduct surveys of public opinion and dissemination of knowledge of important issues.

The website *thenewparadigm.us* is currently staffing with social media coordinators, web designers, web developers, content editors, quality assurance personnel, and project managers. All of these positions are at home and interested persons can send an email to admin@thenewparadigmsolutions.com. If you can't work on your own with minimal direction, don't bother. Keep in mind these are non-profit corporations, so if you require immediate income, don't bother.

Overcoming Opposition

Challenges to *The Best Tax Solution* will come from a disparate collection of special interest groups, from progressives to conservatives and every other group with designs on power, influence, or other peoples money. Lobbyists will lose their influence on malleable politicians. Tax attorneys and tax accountants will lose their jobs. Government employees, especially from the IRS, will lose jobs where they inflict misery on the rest of society. Politicians will protest because they will have to become more transparent to get reelected. Economist will shudder and claim that it is impossible and will not work, mainly because their self-worth is attached to their ego and it is too simple, besides they did not think of it. Large non-profit organizations, like AARP whose majority of income is not from donations, will vehemently oppose based on their "good works", that actually suck money from the poor and middle class. Labor union bosses will also reject any solution that affects their power base, even if it is beneficial to the rank and file.

It may seem like a lot of opposition, but the total amounts to less than 1% of the United States population or about 3 million people. Innovative arguments to counter opposition points as they arise will keep the opposition on defense until the electorate rejects their arguments in favor of *The Best Tax Solution*. Strategies and position papers will be developed to address their anticipated opposition arguments. The goal being not to silence the opposition, but to have the voters come to the conclusion that the opposition arguments are not for the greater good.

Progressive Challenge

Arguments from progressives will be phrased concerning "fair share", "income inequality", "tax breaks for the rich", "child tax credits", or "working families". None of these arguments will be able to stand up to critical debate.

Conservative Challenge

Conservatives will challenge treating passive income as ordinary income, elimination of deductions for extravagant expenses and administrative overhead, and elimination of credits for worthy "investments". One by one they will be exposed as special interest kickbacks.

Lobbyist Challenge

What is the purpose of a lobbyist? What percentage of lobbyists promote social change versus manipulation of the tax code? When *The Best Tax Solution* is implemented, lobbyists will no longer be able to manipulate the tax code because any change in rates would apply equally across the board. Lobbyists should and will be relegated to social issues.

Politician Challenge

Politicians are not the "sharpest knives in the drawer". Publicly, reasons given for not supporting *The Best Tax Solution* will follow an ideology of the progressive or the conservative. Privately, these flawed humans will fear losing power and control. If they think *The Best Tax Solution* will affect their power and control, they will have a conniption fit with *Volume II*. Why should they have power and control, aren't they supposed to represent their constituents? When constituent pressure exceeds that of the lobbyists and their ego, they'll come around or be gone. According to the Constitution the electorate makes the ultimate decision.

Tax Professional Challenge

Many tax preparation companies will cease to exist. Many tax attorneys will change their field of specialty. These people will adapt. The bright side is millions of taxpayers will save billions of hours and billions of dollars. Perhaps these people will create a more productive workforce.

Government Employee Challenge

IRS will loose tens of thousands of jobs during the first 3 years of *The Best Tax Solution* saving the country about 4 billion dollars, not to mention the billions of hours and billions of dollars saved by taxpayers. Through attrition and reassignment these people will easily be absorbed into the workforce, hopefully in more productive and meaningful pursuits.

Federal government unionized workers will receive substantial benefits as described below for any union member. Whether public sector unions are a good idea is addressed in *Volume II*.

Economist Challenge

Obviously, economists may be the hardest to convince because they are "smarter" than other people. Most economists are convinced that some tax expenditures are required for the benefit of society. Why? Where is the evidence that government knows better what to do with your money than you? Where in the Constitution does the government have the right to favor one group over another group? On the contrary, the 14th Amendment guarantees "equal protection".

Economists use theory and modeling systems to predict economic results. Distinction needs to be made to separate the ego of the economist from the theory and the facts. For those that their ego is not an issue, logical analysis should convince some of them.

Non-profit Challenge

Fairness demands that these entities pay their "fair share". Any tax break a non-profit enjoys is nothing other than subsidy from another taxpayer whether they support the mission of the non-profit or not. Where in the Constitution does it require taxpayers to support causes they may not believe in? *The Best Tax Solution* does not tax gifts, so any other revenues should be treated as income or fairness is "out the window".

Labor Union Challenge

Overall, *The Best Tax Solution* greatly benefits union members. Lower rates more than offset the loss of deductions for dues and benefit contributions. Show the membership (they are smarter than you may think) the numbers, and let them decide and not the union bosses.

Pressuring and Convincing Congress and the President

When a critical mass of the electorate is willing to hold their congressperson accountable, then passage of *The Best Tax Solution* can become a reality. What does critical mass look like? Critical mass can be realized with as few as 269 people influenced by fewer than 1,000 people. You may ask how can 269 individuals pass *The Best Tax Solution*? Do the math. Of 435 members of the House of Representatives, 218 are needed to pass a bill. Of the 100 members of the Senate, 50 are needed to pass the bill with vote of the Vice President at the direction of the President. To avoid a filibuster this can be accomplished through budget reconciliation. 218 Representatives plus 50 Senators plus one President is 269. Are you willing to be one of the 1,000? If so send an email to admin@thenewparadigmsolutions.com.

Appendix A - Words and Phrases No Longer Needed with The Best Tax Solution

A
Absence
Abusive
Academic
Accelerated
Accident
Accrue
Accumulate
Achievement
Acquisition
Active
Activity
Acts
Actuarial
Additional Requirement
Additional Tax
Adjusted
Adjusted Gross Income
Adjusted Taxable Income
Adjusted Basis
Adjustment
Adopted
Adoption
Advance
Advertising
Affiliated Group
Aggregation
Agreement
Agriculture
Aid
Aircraft
Airplane
Airport
Alcohol
Alimony
Allocation
Allocation Formula
Allowable
Allowed
Almond
Alternative
Alternative Minimum

Tax
Ambulance
Amortization
Amtrak
Amusement
Annexed
Annualized
Annuitant
Annuity
Anti-abuse
Anti-churning
Appliances
Applicable
Applicable Amount
Applicable Percentage
Applicable Severance
Apportion
Appraised
Appraisal
Appreciation
Appropriate
Approval
Approval Requirement
Arbitrage
Archer MSA
Architectural
Armed Forces
Arrangement
Artist
Assessment
Assets
Assign
Assignment
Assistance
Assistants
Association
Assumed
Assumption
Astronaut
Athletic
Attribution
Author
Automobile

Average
Avoidance
Awards

B
Bank
Bank Holding Company
Barrier
Base Amount
Base Period
Basis
Beginning
Beneficiary
Beverage
Bicycle
Black Lung
Blighted
Blindness
Boats
Boiler
Bona fide
Bond
Book
Borne
Borrow
Burial
Bus
Business Leagues
Business Use
Building

C
Cafeteria Plan
Camp
Campus
Canada
Cancel
Cap
Capacity
Capital
Capital Loss
Capitalize
Care
Carrying Charges

Carrybacks
Carryforward
Carryovers
Cash Flow
Cash Value
Casualty Loss
Catch
Catch-up
Ceiling
Cellular Telephone
Cellulosic Biofuel
Census
Certain
Chambers of Commerce
Change of Ownership
Character
Charitable
Chemical
Children
Chronic
Church
Churning
Circulation
Citrus
Civil Tax
Civilian
Clarification
Class
Classification
Clean
Clean Air Act
Clean-burning Fuel
Clinical
Closure
Clothing
Coal
Collectively Bargained
Combat Zone
Commercial
Commissioned
Commodity
Community
Community Property

Appendix A - Words and Phrases No Longer Needed with The Best Tax Solution

Commuter
Commuting
Compete
Component
Composite
Computer
Condition
Confidential
Connection
Consent
Conservation
Consistent
Consolidated
Earnings
Contract
Contribution
Construction
Construction Period
Constructive
Ownership
Constructively
Consumer Price
Index (CPI)
Contaminated
Contemporaneous
Contour Furrowing
Contract
Contribution
Control
Control Group
Convention
Conversion
Converted
Convertible Stock
Cooling
Cooperative
Coordination
Copyright
Corporate Preference
Item
Cosmetic
Cost Depletion
Cost-of-living
Cost-sharing
County

Couple
Covenant
Coverage
Creative
Credit
Credit Unions
Crew
Criteria
Crude Oil
Crop
Cruise Ship
Currency
Customer
Cut-off

D

Damage
Day Care
De Minimis Rule
Deafness
Death
Death Tax
Debenture
Debt
Debt Exchange
Debt Instrument
Debt Service
Decedent
Declare
Declining Balance
Method
Decommission
Decrease
Dedication
Deductible
Deduction
Deed
Deemed
Deferral
Deferral Period
Delay
Demolition
Demonstrate
Denial
Dental

Department
Dependent
Depletion
Deposit
Depreciation
Designate
Destroy
Development Costs
Dies
Diesel Fuel
Different
Diminish
Dinner
Direct
Directors
Disability
Disallowance
Disaster
Discharge of
Indebtedness
Discount
Discrimination
Discriminatory
Disposal
Disposition
Disproportionate
Disqualified
Disqualified
Individual
Disregarded
Distribution
District
Ditch
Diversion Channels
Divorce
Dock
Domestic
Domestic Relation
Donee
Donor
Double
Double Benefit
Drainage Ditches
Drilling Costs
Drug

Dues
Duration
Dwelling Unit

E

Earned Income
Earnings
Earthen Dams
Eating
Economic Life
Education
Effective
Efficient
Effort
Elderly
Election
Electricity
Eligible
Emergency
Employee-Owner
Employee Use
Employment Credit
Empowerment Zone
Endangered Species
Endowment
Energy
Enhancement
Enjoyment
Entertainment
Enrollment
Environmental
Environmental
Protection Agency
(EPA)
Equal
Equity
Erosion
Establishment
Estate
Estate Tax
Ethanol
Exception
Excess
Excess of Basis
Exchange

Appendix A - Words and Phrases No Longer Needed with The Best Tax Solution

Excludable
Exclusion
Exclusive
Exempt
Exemption
Existing
Expanded
Expatriate
Expenditure
Expense
Experimental
Exploration
Export
Expropriation
Extension
Extraordinary

F
Face-amount
Facility
Failure
Fair Market Value (FMV)
Fair Rental
Family
Family Units
Farm
Farmland
Federal Home Loan Bank
Federal Hours of Service
Federally-subsidized
Feedstock
Fertilizer
Film
Financed
Financial Institution
Financing
Fire
Firefighters
First In First Out (FIFO)
First-time
Fiscal Year

Fish
Flexible
Flowed
Flow-through
Food
Foreign Corporation
Foreign Move
Forestry
Forfeiture
Formation
Former
Foster
Fraction
Fractional
Franchises
Free-lance
Freight
Fringe
Fuel
Funding
Furnishing
Furniture

G
Gain
Gambling
Gas
Gasification
Gear
General Rule
Generation Skipping
Geothermal
Gift
Gift Tax
Golden Parachute
Good Faith
Goodwill
Gospel
Governmental
Governor
Grant
Green Building
Gross Income
Gross Vehicle Weight
Group

Grove
Grow
Guarantee

H
Handicapped
Harmless
Harvest
Hazardous
Head-of-household
Health
Hearse
Heating
Hedge
Helicopter
High
High-speed
Higher
Higher Education
Highly Compensated
Highway
Historic Structure
Holder
Holding Company
Holding Period
Home Rule City
Homebuyer
Horticultural
Hospital
Household
Housing
Hunting
Hydrocarbon
Hydroelectric
Hydrogen

I
Ice Skating
Immediate
Impairment
Import
Imposed
Improvement
In General
In Lieu Of

Inadequate
Inaugural
Incidental
Includible Compensation
Income Forecast Method
Income Limit
Increase
Increment
Incurred
Indebtedness
Indian
Indirect
Industrial
Ineligible
Inflation
Infrastructure
Infringe
Inheritance
Injectant
Injury
Innovation
Insolvent
Installed
Internal Revenue Service
Installment
Institution
Insurance
Intangible
Integrated Oil Company
Intellectual
Intelligence
Intentional
Interim
Intercity
Intragroup Stock
Inure
Institutions
Inventory
Involuntary
Iron
Irrespective

Appendix A - Words and Phrases No Longer Needed with The Best Tax Solution

Irrevocable
Irrigation
Issuance
Issue
Itemize

J
Joint
Joint Return
Jurisdiction
Jury

K
Key Employee
Key Person
Killed

L
Land
Last In First Out (LIFO)
Lease
Legal
Lending Company
Leveling
Liabilities
License
Licensing
Life
Lifetime
Lighting
Like-kind
Limitation
Limited Liability Corporation
Linens
Liquid
Listed Property
Livestock
Loan
Lobbyist
Location
Lodging
Look-back Method
Loophole

Long-term
Loss
Loss Carrybacks
Lost
Low-income
Low Sulfur
Lowest
Lump-sum
Lunch
Luxury
Luxury Water Transportation

M
Management
Manner
Manufacture
Marine
Marital Status
Marketing
Married
Mass
Maturity
Maximum
Meal
Median Family Income
Medical
Medical Savings Account (MSA)
Medicine
Member
Mental
Merchant
Methanol
Method
Method of Accounting
Metropolitan
Mexico
Mileage
Military Housing
Mineral
Mineral Exploration
Mine Rescue

Minimum
Minister
Minority
Mitigation
Modification
Modified
Monthly
Moody's
Mortgage
Motor Vehicle
Motorsports
Moving
Multiple Inclusions
Municipal
Municipalities
Musical Works
Mutual

N
Native Alaskan
Natural Gas
Natural Person
Net
Net Operating Loss (NOL)
Network
New
Nominal
Non-profit
Non-corporation
Non-deductible
Non-deferral Period
Non-individual
Non-recognition
Nonresident
Nontaxable Earnings
Normalization
North American Area
Notification
Nuclear Powerplants
Numerical
Nutrition

O
Obligations

Occupant
Occupancy
Officer
Oil
Operation
Opportunity
Option
Optional
Ordinary Income
Ore
Original
Ornamental Trees
Otherwise
Out-of-pocket
Outlets
Output
Outstanding
Overlapping
Owner
Owner-occupied
Ownership

P
Pacific Islands
Parachute Payment
Parent
Parking
Parsonage
Partial
Partial Liquidation
Participant
Participate
Partnership
Parts
Pass-thru
Passenger
Patent
Patrons
Payment
Per Diem
Perform
Peripheral Equipment
Period
Period for Distribution

Appendix A - Words and Phrases No Longer Needed with The Best Tax Solution

Periodic
Permitted
Personal Holding Company
Personal Service Corporation
Personal Use
Petroleum
Phase-in
Phase-out
Phone
Photographer
Physician
Placed in Service
Plan
Plant
Planted
Pledge
Policy
Policyholder
Political Candidates
Political Party
Pollution Control
Pooled
Population
Portfolio
Portion
Possession
Pre-death
Predecessor
Predominantly
Preferred Stock
Preference
Premature
Premises
Premium
Prepayment
Preproductive
Prescribed
Prescription
Present Value
Preservation
Presumption
Previously
Price Inflation

Primary
Principal
Principal Residence
Prisoner
Prisoners of War (POW)
Private
Private Foundations
Prizes
Pro Rata
Proceeds
Product
Production
Profit
Program
Prohibited
Project
Projected Earnings
Property
Property Transfers
Proportionate
Proposed
Protection
Provision
Proximity
Public
Public-private
Public Property
Public School
Public Utility
Puerto Rico
Purchase
Purpose

Q

Qualified
Qualified Business
Qualified Business Use
Qualified Minority
Qualified Ownership
Qualified Plans
Qualified Small Issuer
Qualified Trade

R

Racquet Sports
Rail
Railroad
Raised
Rancher
Ratio
Ratio of Debt to Equity
Real Estate Boards
Realized
Reacquired
Redevelopment
Reform
Refuel
Rehabilitation
Remove
Realignment
Reason
Reasonable
Reasonable Compensation
Recapture
Receivable
Receipt
Recognized
Re-contributed
Record-keeping
Recovery
Recovery Period
Recreation
Recycle
Redemption
Reduce
Reduction
Refinancing
Refinery
Reflect
Reforestation
Refunding
Regardless
Regulatory Authority
Rehabilitation
Reimburse

Reinsurance
Related Corporation
Related Individual
Related Person
Related Terminal Income
Related Terminal Service
Relationship
Relatives
Relief
Remediation
Removable
Renewable
Rent
Rental Period
Rental Use
Repaid
Repayable
Research
Reservation
Reserve
Reservist
Reservoir
Residual
Response
Retainage
Retention
Reorganization
Requirement
Replacement
Representative
Repurchase
Research
Reserve
Residence
Residential
Restaurant
Restrictions
Retail
Retirement
Retrofit
Revitalization
Revocation
Risk

Appendix A - Words and Phrases No Longer Needed with The Best Tax Solution

Rollover
Rounding
Rural

S
S Corporation
Safe Harbor
Sale-leasebacks
Salvage Value
Sanctioned
Satellite
Satisfy
Savings
Savings Bond
Scholarship
School
Scientific
Scope
Scrap
Securities
Security
Self-insured
Seller
Separate
Separations
Series
Serviceman
Set Aside
Settlement
Sewage
Share
Shared Equity
Shareholder
Shipowner
Short Sale
Short-term
Sick
Sick Pay
Single-family
Site
Size
Skewed
Sky-boxes
Small
Small Business

Small Employer
Smart Grid
Software
Solid
Soil
Sound Recordings
Soundness
Source of Gain/Loss
Spacecraft
Special
Special Interest
Special Needs
Special Rule
Sport Utility Vehicle (SUV)
Sports
Spouse
Square Footage
Stapled Entity
Start-up
State
Statistical
Steel
Stock
Stock Rights
Storage
Storage Fees
Storage Use
Straddle
Straight Line Method
Structure
Student
Student Loan
Sub-Chapter S
Subordinate
Subprime
Subsequent
Subsidiary
Subsidy
Substance
Substantially Equivalent
Substantiation
Substituted
Supplemental

Supplier
Surgeon
Surgery
Surtax
Survivor
Sustainable
Syndication

T
Tangible
Target
Targeted
Tax Break
Tax Credit
Tax Exempt
Tax-Free
Taxable
Taxable Income
Taxable Year
Taxidermy
Teaching
Technology
Telecommunications Equipment
Telephone
Television
Temporary
Tenant
Terminal Railroad Corporation
Terminate
Terrorists
Tertiary
Test
Testing
Tickets
Tier
Timber
Tract
Trade
Training
Training Credit
Transferred
Transit Pass
Transition

Transmission
Transmitted
Transportation
Travel Expenses
Treated
Treaties
Treatment
Trip
Troubled Assets Relief Program (TARP)
Truck
Trust
Trustee
Tuition
Tunnel
Turbine

U
Unborrowed
Undistributed
Unemployment
Unforeseeable
Unharvested
Uniformed
Uninsured
Unloaded Gross Vehicle Weight
Unrecovered Basis
Unrecovered Losses
Unused
Urban
Use of Proceeds
Used
Useful Life
Utilities

V
Valuable Consideration
Valuation
Value
Van
Vehicle
Veteran

Appendix A - Words and Phrases No Longer Needed with The Best Tax Solution

Viatical
Victims
Video Tape
Windfall
Volume
Volume Cap
Volunteer

W
Wage
Waiver
Waste
Water
Watercourses
Weapons
Wells
Wetland
Whaling
Wharves
Whistleblower
Wholesome
Wildlife
Windbreaks
Workers
Compensation
Working Abroad
Write-off
Writer
Written

Y
Yield